Obesity

Other Books of Related Interest:

GLOBALVIEWPOINTS

Obesity

Margaret Haerens, Book Editor

GREENHAVEN PRESS
A part of Gale, Cengage Learning

GALE
CENGAGE Learning®

Detroit • New York • San Francisco • New Haven, Conn • Waterville, Maine • London

GALE
CENGAGE Learning·

Elizabeth Des Chenes, *Managing Editor*

© 2012 Greenhaven Press, a part of Gale, Cengage Learning

Gale and Greenhaven Press are registered trademarks used herein under license.

For more information, contact:
Greenhaven Press
27500 Drake Rd.
Farmington Hills, MI 48331-3535
Or you can visit our Internet site at gale.cengage.com

For product information and technology assistance, contact us at

Gale Customer Support, 1-800-877-4253
For permission to use material from this text or product, submit all requests online at
www.cengage.com/permissions

Further permissions questions can be emailed to permissionrequest@cengage.com

Articles in Greenhaven Press anthologies are often edited for length to meet page requirements. In addition, original titles of these works are changed to clearly present the main thesis and to explicitly indicate the author's opinion. Every effort is made to ensure that Greenhaven Press accurately reflects the original intent of the authors. Every effort has been made to trace the owners of copyrighted material.

Cover image copyright © Ryan Pyle/Corbis.

LIBRARY OF CONGRESS CATALOGING-IN-PUBLICATION DATA

Obesity / edited by Margaret Haerens.
    p. cm. -- (Global viewpoints)
Summary: "Obesity: The Global Obesity Epidemic; Obesity Factors; Obesity Effects; Anti-Obesity Policies"-- Provided by publisher.
    Includes bibliographical references and index.
    ISBN 978-0-7377-5660-9 (hardback) -- ISBN 978-0-7377-5661-6 (paperback)
  1. Obesity--Juvenile literature. I. Haerens, Margaret.
    RC628.O2145 2011
    616.3'98--dc23

                                                          2011027148

Printed in Mexico
1 2 3 4 5 6 7 15 14 13 12 11

Contents

Chapter 1: The Global Obesity Epidemic

Chapter 2: Obesity Factors

Mauritania's culture of beauty dictates that very young girls are force-fed until they become obese. Older women turn to dangerous appetite-inducing drugs to keep their weight up. As they age, women in Mauritania develop weight-related diseases, like diabetes and hypertension. The government is countering obesity by underscoring the dangers of it and presenting thin role models on TV, in movies, and in song.

Many Pakistani students develop disordered eating habits that lead to obesity and weight-related diseases. The convenience and availability of fast food is a major component of the growing obesity problem in the country, especially for young students in urban areas. There should be mandatory nutrition classes for all students to set them on the right path.

Chapter 3: Obesity Effects

Chapter 4: Anti-Obesity Policies

There is no political push in Canada to post calorie counts for fast food, like they do in the United States. Part of the problem is a well-funded lobbying group, the Canadian Restaurant and Foodservices Association, which has fought strongly against such measures. The debate over calorie counts is key considering the obesity epidemic in Canada.

Foreword

"The problems of all of humanity can only be solved by all of humanity."
—*Swiss author Friedrich Dürrenmatt*

Global interdependence has become an undeniable reality. Mass media and technology have increased worldwide access to information and created a society of global citizens. Understanding and navigating this global community is a challenge, requiring a high degree of information literacy and a new level of learning sophistication.

Building on the success of its flagship series, Opposing Viewpoints, Greenhaven Press has created the Global Viewpoints series to examine a broad range of current, often controversial topics of worldwide importance from a variety of international perspectives. Providing students and other readers with the information they need to explore global connections and think critically about worldwide implications, each Global Viewpoints volume offers a panoramic view of a topic of widespread significance.

Drugs, famine, immigration—a broad, international treatment is essential to do justice to social, environmental, health, and political issues such as these. Junior high, high school, and early college students, as well as general readers, can all use Global Viewpoints anthologies to discern the complexities relating to each issue. Readers will be able to examine unique national perspectives while, at the same time, appreciating the interconnectedness that global priorities bring to all nations and cultures.

Material in each volume is selected from a diverse range of sources, including journals, magazines, newspapers, nonfiction books, speeches, government documents, pamphlets, organization newsletters, and position papers. Global Viewpoints is truly global, with material drawn primarily from international sources available in English and secondarily from US sources with extensive international coverage.

Features of each volume in the Global Viewpoints series include:

- An **annotated table of contents** that provides a brief summary of each essay in the volume, including the name of the country or area covered in the essay.

- An **introduction** specific to the volume topic.

- A **world map** to help readers locate the countries or areas covered in the essays.

- For each viewpoint, an **introduction** that contains notes about the author and source of the viewpoint explains why material from the specific country is being presented, summarizes the main points of the viewpoint, and offers three **guided reading questions** to aid in understanding and comprehension.

- **For further discussion** questions that promote critical thinking by asking the reader to compare and contrast aspects of the viewpoints or draw conclusions about perspectives and arguments.

- A worldwide list of **organizations to contact** for readers seeking additional information.

- A **periodical bibliography** for each chapter and a **bibliography of books** on the volume topic to aid in further research.

- A comprehensive **subject index** to offer access to people, places, events, and subjects cited in the text, with the countries covered in the viewpoints highlighted.

Global Viewpoints is designed for a broad spectrum of readers who want to learn more about current events, history, political science, government, international relations, economics, environmental science, world cultures, and sociology— students doing research for class assignments or debates, teachers and faculty seeking to supplement course materials, and others wanting to understand current issues better. By presenting how people in various countries perceive the root causes, current consequences, and proposed solutions to worldwide challenges, Global Viewpoints volumes offer readers opportunities to enhance their global awareness and their knowledge of cultures worldwide.

Introduction

> *"Obesity is a complex condition, one with serious social and psychological dimensions, that affects virtually all age and socioeconomic groups and threatens to overwhelm both developed and developing countries."*
>
> —World Health Organization

Many experts agree with the World Health Organization (WHO) that obesity is a serious global epidemic that affects both developed and developing countries. According to WHO, approximately 1.5 billion adults over the age of twenty were obese or overweight in 2008; that means more than one in ten of the world's adult population were afflicted. It is also a crisis among the world's children. In 2010 43 million children under the age of five were classified as obese. Unfortunately, these rates are expected to get even worse. WHO predicts that the number of obese or overweight adults in the world will climb to 2.3 billion by 2015.

Experts worry that these exploding rates of global obesity are leading to a public health care crisis. As more and more people around the world become obese or overweight, the rate of weight-related diseases will increase, including type 2 diabetes, sleep apnea, hypertension, and heart disease. In many countries, this puts an immense financial strain on government-funded health systems, hospitals, and other health providers, as medical professionals struggle to find resources to curb the rising rates of obesity and treat those with weight-related diseases in their communities. In Great Britain, for example, experts predict that the costs of the obesity epidemic will cripple the country's National Health Service. In the

United States, a 2010 study by the Center on Social Dynamics and Policy found that the health care costs of obesity may total up to $147 billion annually.

By the end of the twentieth century, national and local governments began to formulate a wide range of policies to effectively address the issue of obesity. Weight, once thought to be the responsibility of the individual, was often classified as a public health matter and therefore subject to government intervention.

One of the earliest measures to address obesity and over-weight was nutritional labeling, which is required on packaged foods sold in markets. The labels list the number of calories per serving, as well as total fat, sodium, carbohydrates, protein, and other nutritional ingredients. Such information is considered useful for consumers looking to monitor their weight and be informed of the nutritional value of their food purchases. In the United States, a law was passed requiring nutritional labeling in 1990. Canada passed its own nutritional labeling law in 2003, and Mexico has had one since 1996. Many other countries in the world have some form of nutritional labeling.

In 2008 New York City passed a pioneering law taking food labeling a step further when it became the first US city to require fast-food restaurants to post calorie counts for consumers, a practice known as menu labeling. A number of other states and municipalities, including San Francisco and Seattle, followed. Other countries are also considering a menu labeling law, particularly for fast-food outlets.

While nutritional and menu labeling are meant to inform consumers about the foods they are consuming, other legislation is meant to protect consumers. Banning trans fat is one such measure that has garnered attention in recent years. Trans fat is a particularly dangerous type of unsaturated fat that can lead to heart disease and obesity. In 2003 Denmark became the first country to strictly regulate the sale of foods containing trans fat, with the aim of reducing obesity and heart disease. Switzerland followed, and several other countries initiated a voluntary ban on trans fat. In the United States, several major cities adopted various restrictions on trans fat, including New York City, Philadelphia, Boston, and Chicago. In 2008 California became the first US state to ban the use of trans fat in foods served in restaurants.

Other legislation under consideration includes adding a tax on certain kinds of foods that contribute to the obesity epidemic. Many countries and communities take the money raised from such taxes and apply it to health programs to fight obesity and treat weight-related diseases. It is thought that these taxes will discourage the consumption of unhealthy foods and drinks. One popular tax is on soft drinks and other sugary beverages. In 2009 the American Heart Association stated that soft drinks and sugar-sweetened drinks were the largest source of added sugars in American diets. As a result, New York City and other US communities considered a soda tax. In Denmark, the government imposed not only a tax on soda, but also a tax on chocolate and candy in 2010. In Romania, a tax on fast food was introduced that same year—the first of its kind in the world. A year later, Hungary introduced a "hamburger tax," which adds a tax to all unhealthy food and drinks, including fast food.

There are a number of other policies that governments have employed to fight the obesity epidemic. In Canada, the government offers a children's fitness tax credit that allows parents to claim up to $500 a year for their children's fitness expenses. In France, the government removed all vending machines from schools and emphasized physical activity and healthier school meals. In the United States, politicians are considering subsidizing healthier foods to make them more affordable and increasing food stamp funds for fruits and vegetables. Soft drink machines were removed from many American schools, as health officials were particularly concerned about children and their access to sugary beverages. In 2010 First Lady Michelle Obama initiated the "Let's Move!" campaign, which aimed at curbing the childhood obesity crisis in the United States and culminated in the signing of the Healthy, Hunger-Free Kids Act of 2010, a law that improved the nutritional quality of school lunches in America. In Mauritania, where obese women are glorified, the government launched a campaign to inform women about the dangers of obesity and provide thin role models to counteract prevailing cultural ideals of overweight and obese women.

The most extreme legislative response to the obesity epidemic may be Japan's obesity law. Passed in 2008, the law sets a government-imposed maximum waistline size for any Japanese adult over the age of forty at 33.5 inches for men and 35.4 inches for women. If an individual's waistline is larger than those maximums, the company he or she works for will be fined, and the individual might be required to go for weight counseling.

The authors of the viewpoints presented in *Global Viewpoints: Obesity* explore various aspects of the global obesity epidemic. The information provided in this volume offers insight into the factors that cause global obesity; investigate its economic, political, and social implications; and examine the ways that various countries and local communities are confronting the crisis.

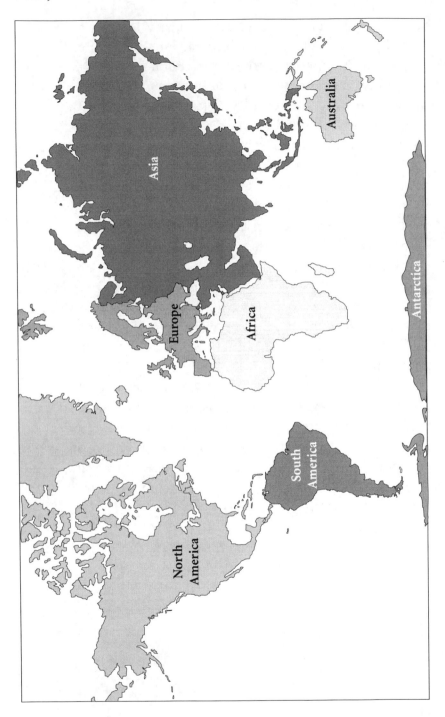

The Global
Obesity Epidemic

Obesity Is a Global Crisis

International Association for the Study of Obesity

The International Association for the Study of Obesity is a non-profit organization that links state and regional associations and health and wellness professionals interested in the latest news on obesity. In the following viewpoint, the organization surveys the global obesity problem and elucidates the economic and social toll the condition takes on individuals and communities. The organization concludes that obesity is putting an intolerable strain on health care and social resources in a number of countries.

As you read, consider the following questions:

1. According to the viewpoint, how many adults worldwide are too fat?
2. How many school-age children are overweight globally, as cited by the author?
3. What percentage of their health care budgets do European nations spend on obesity, according to the author?

The epidemic of obesity is now recognized as one of the most important public health problems facing the world today. Tragically, adult obesity is more common globally than undernutrition. There are around 475 million obese adults with over twice that number overweight—that means around 1.5 billion adults are too fat. Over 200 million school-age children are overweight, making this generation the first predicted to have a shorter life span than their parents.

Understanding Obesity

What is obesity? Obesity is a medical condition described as excess body weight in the form of fat. When accumulated, this fat can lead to severe health impairments.

What causes obesity? Obesity is caused by an energy imbalance; when intake of calories exceeds expenditure of calories, the surplus energy is stored as body weight. There are a multitude of 'obesogenic' factors contributing to the increased energy consumption and decreased energy expenditure that are responsible for obesity, including:

- Declining levels of physical labour as populations move from rural to urban settings and abandon walking in favour of driving, labour-saving devices in the home, and the replacement of active sport and play by television and computer games.

- Higher levels of food consumption, or an increase in energy density (particularly fat content) of the food we eat.

- Social, economic, educational and cultural factors are important underlying causes of obesity, although how they inter-relate to promote or protect against the development of obesity is complex and varies considerably by country.

Defining Obesity

How is obesity measured? The most widely used method of measuring and identifying obesity is Body Mass Index (BMI). BMI = weight in kg/height in m2.

Overweight, or pre-obesity, is defined as a BMI of 25–29.9 kg/m2, while a BMI >30 kg/m2 defines obesity. These BMI thresholds were proposed by WHO [World Health Organization] expert reports and reflect the increasing health risk of excess weight as BMI increases above an optimal range of

21–23 kg/m2, the recommended median goal for adult Caucasian populations (WHO/NUT/NCD, 2000).

While BMI is a simple measure that is very useful for populations, it should be considered a rough guide for predicting risk in individuals. The distribution and amount of body fat are also crucial determinants of some obesity-associated health risks. Visceral fat, particularly in the abdominal region, has a stronger association with type 2 diabetes and cardiovascular disease than BMI. Accordingly, measures of central obesity such as waist:hip ratio and waist circumference provide more robust indices of overall obesity-related health risk than BMI alone.

Health Impact of Obesity

Obesity is an important cause of morbidity, disability and premature death (WHO, 2004). Obesity increases the risk for a wide range of chronic diseases; BMI is thought to account for about 60% of the risk of developing type 2 diabetes, over 20% of that for hypertension and coronary heart disease, and between 10 and 30% for various cancers. Other co-morbidities include gall bladder disease, fatty liver, sleep apnoea and osteoarthritis.

The disability attributable to obesity and its consequences in 2004 was calculated at over 36 million disability-adjusted life years (DALYs), due primarily to ischaemic [a restriction of blood supply] heart disease and type 2 diabetes (WHO Global Health Risks Report, 2004).

Obesity shortens life expectancy. In 2004, increased BMI alone was estimated to account for 2.8 million deaths, while the combined total with physical inactivity was 6.0 million (WHO Global Health Risks Report, 2004)—surpassing the excess mortality associated with tobacco, and approaching that of high blood pressure, the top risk factor for death.

Relationships between obesity and health risks vary between populations. Asians, for example, are more susceptible and thus BMI risk thresholds are lower than other populations, with an action point for overweight defined at 23 kg/m2.

Obesity in Children Childhood obesity is already common, especially in westernized countries. In 2004, according to IOTF [International Obesity TaskForce] criteria, it was estimated that ∼10% of children worldwide aged 5–17 years were overweight and that 2–3% were obese (Lebstein et al., 2004). Prevalence rates vary considerably between different regions and countries, from <5% in Africa and parts of Asia to >20% in Europe and >30% in the Americas and some countries in the Middle East. Becoming obese earlier in life clearly amplifies certain health risks, particularly for type 2 diabetes.

Social Impact of Obesity

For individuals, psychological problems associated with obesity are common, wide-ranging and potentially serious. Growing worldwide awareness of obesity may have reinforced prejudice against the obese, who are often stigmatized. Depression and low self-esteem can affect an individual's quality of life, mental health, educational achievement and employment prospects. Cultural and ethnic factors undoubtedly modulate the social impact of obesity, as well as its perception. In some parts of the world—notably the Pacific Islands and parts of Africa—obesity may still carry historic and cultural connotations of power, beauty and affluence.

Growing worldwide awareness of obesity may have reinforced prejudice against the obese, who are often stigmatized.

Costs of Obesity

Obesity has substantial direct and indirect costs that put a strain on healthcare and social resources.

Percentage of Adult Population That Is Obese

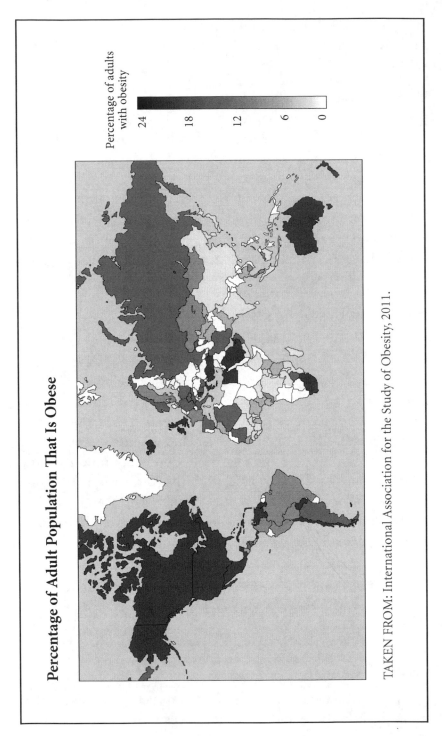

Percentage of adults
with obesity

24

18

12

6

0

TAKEN FROM: International Association for the Study of Obesity, 2011.

Direct medical costs include preventative, diagnostic and treatment services related to overweight and associated co-morbidities. European nations spend 2–8% of their health care budgets on obesity, equating to 0.6% of gross domestic product (GDP) for some (Müller-Riemenschneider, Reinhold, Berghöfer, and Willich, 2008). In the USA, estimates based on 2008 data indicated that overweight and obesity account for $147 billion in total medical expenditure (Finkelstein, Trogdon, Cohen and Dietz, 2009). Although indirect costs to society can be substantially higher, they are often neglected. They relate to income lost from decreased productivity, reduced opportunities and restricted activity, illness, absenteeism and premature death. In addition, there are high costs associated with the numerous infrastructure changes that societies must make to cope with obese people (i.e., reinforced beds, operating tables and wheelchairs; enlarged turnstiles and seats in sports-grounds, and modifications to transport safety standards).

Obesity is now reaching pandemic proportions across much of the world, and its consequences are set to impose unprecedented health, financial and social burdens on global society, unless effective actions are taken to reverse the trend.

Ugandan Rates of Obesity Are Increasing

Lominda Afedraru

Lominda Afedraru is a writer for the Daily Monitor. *In the following viewpoint, she reports that recent demographic surveys reveal that obesity is on the rise in Uganda, making it a country affected by both malnutrition and overnutrition. Afedraru states that conditions vary in the country because of different eating habits and changes in technology where food is being processed.*

As you read, consider the following questions:

1. As stated by Afedraru, what percentage of Uganda's population is obese?
2. According to the World Health Organization, what are the top two noncommunicable diseases in the world?
3. Why is obesity more prevalent in western Uganda, according to the government official quoted by Afedraru?

A recent demographic survey carried out throughout the country has shown that 10 percent of Uganda's population is obese and these include children and adults.

Prof. James Ntambi, a specialist in biochemistry, has for the last 20 years been conducting research on obesity which was previously regarded as a problem common in the Western world but is slowly increasing among the African population, including Uganda.

Lominda Afedraru, "Obesity on the Increase," *The Daily Monitor*, October 9, 2010. Reproduced by permission.

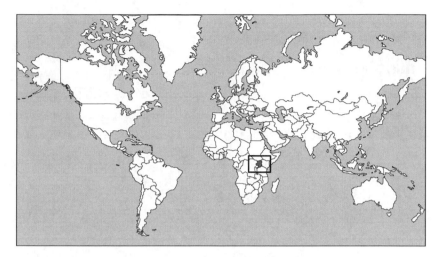

Obesity is a metabolic disorder resulting from chronic imbalance between energy uptake and its expenditure by the body, and it requires a lifelong treatment for control purposes because it cannot be treated completely.

Other factors causing this imbalance are uncontrolled food consumption, sedentary lifestyles, the environment in which people live and health care organisation of the country.

Obesity is a metabolic disorder resulting from chronic imbalance between energy uptake and its expenditure by the body, and it requires a lifelong treatment for control purposes because it cannot be treated completely.

Prof. Ntambi has been carrying out the research at Makerere University's department of Biochemistry and Molecular Biology and later moved to the US to continue with the study at Johns Hopkins University and University of Wisconsin.

He said according to the World Health Organization's 2010 statistics, the leading cause of death worldwide is cancer but among the noncommunicable diseases influenza is number one worldwide, followed by obesity, coronary heart disease, liver disease, asthma and alcoholism among others. Prof.

Ntambi said the magnitude of obesity has affected children in 94 countries including Uganda.

Child Obesity

"In Uganda we have child obesity as well as malnutrition. The disease cuts across all ages, race, ethnic groups and both genders and it is becoming rampant due to changes in technology where most consumed food is now being processed," Prof. Ntambi said.

He was addressing a cross section of stakeholders in a public dialogue organised by the Uganda National Academy of Sciences recently in Kampala on the relationship between genetics nutrition and noncommunicable diseases. Apart from USA and Africa, other countries affected by obesity include England, Maribus, Australia and Brazil.

The US government according to Prof. Ntambi in 2009 spent Shs 117 billion for treating people with obesity. The deputy principal of Makerere College of Health Sciences, Prof. John Tuhe Kakitahi, agreed that there is an increase of obesity in the country but said the distribution is uneven due to the different eating habits of people.

High Blood Pressure

He said cases have been identified mostly in western Uganda where they tend to eat fatty foods. "From the recent democratic survey by health science researchers, apart from adults having the disease, some children have been identified with it. We have gone to the communities but it is on the increase although people used to think it is a disease for the rich," Prof. Kakitahi said.

He said those who are obese are likely to develop high blood pressure, cancer, diabetes and already those who are overweight in Uganda are rated at 3 per cent.

However, Prof. Ntambi's research in two American universities involved the use of mice genes since it is difficult to conduct the tests on humans.

Obesity and Malnutrition

Nutritionists ... advise that in order to combat malnutrition and its subsequent longer term effects, efforts should be made to improve the nutrition of [a] child even before its mother conceives through proper feeding and other healthy practices. The situation analysis says that about 11 per cent of children are born already stunted and about 16 per cent are likely to be wasted at birth.

"Your Eating Habits Might Lead to Your Last Breath-Experts,"
Daily Monitor, *September 12, 2010.*

They picked two mice, a normal type and a mutant one and manipulated their genes for the study. "We did one manipulation where we took one type of the normal mouse which lives in the bush and one mutant type. We gave them various types of food with different diets. We discovered that the mutant type of mouse eats as much but did not gain weight," Prof. Ntambi explained.

Lab Tests

"We created animals which eat as much but did not gain weight, then we introduced the gene of the mutant mouse into that animal which lacked leptin and it did suffer from obesity. This is how we determined the same thing to be happening with human beings," he added.

He said not all overweight people are obese but a person suffers from obesity when fat produced from their body begins to stay in the blood vessel which is supposed to contain blood. The fat then blocks the heart, making it not to function well.

He said the hormone which controls obesity is called leptin and once someone lacks this hormone, he or she is likely to become obese because he may fail to control his appetite.

Leptin deficiency in human beings according to Prof. Ntambi leads to drastic increase in obesity although there are very few people in the world who lack this hormone.

Those who suffer from obesity as a result of lack of leptin can be treated by injecting the hormone in them but the reaction depends on one's genes. Other people are advised to take slimming pills and cholesterol leveling drugs, while others are advised to do physical exercise and have nutritional diet as well as positive energy balance.

Prof. Ntambi said to prevent obesity people must observe that the energy that goes in them must be equal to the energy coming out.

Australia Has a Major Obesity Crisis

Ross Gittins

Ross Gittins is the economics editor for the Sydney Morning Herald. *In the following viewpoint, he examines the findings of the 2010 Organisation for Economic Co-operation and Development report that confirms that obesity is becoming a top public health concern in Australia and around the world. Gittins contends that obesity is a direct result of the success of capitalism and technological advances that make food production and processing easier, and society must now realistically confront the problem in a constructive manner.*

As you read, consider the following questions:

1. What percentage of adults are overweight or obese in Australia, as stated in the viewpoint?
2. According to the viewpoint, how much is Australia's overweight rate predicted to rise in the next ten years?
3. What is the definition of "sweet spot," as used in the viewpoint?

I have bad news and good about the O-word. Although there has been a suggestion in some quarters that the media got overexcited about the "obesity epidemic", a report from the Organisation for Economic Co-operation and Develop-

Ross Gittins, "Obesity Problem Is Bigger than We Think, Despite GDP Benefits," *National Times*, October 6, 2010. Reproduced by permission of the author.

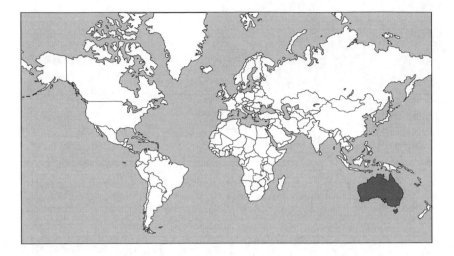

ment [OECD]—unlikely to be a purveyor of faddish enthusi-asms—has confirmed the seriousness of the problem.

The report says obesity is worsening throughout the developed world and becoming the top public health concern. One in two people is now overweight or obese in almost half the developed countries. In some, two out of three people will be in trouble within 10 years.

In Australia, 61 per cent of adults are overweight or obese, making us almost as fat as the Americans. In 20 years, our overweight rate has risen faster than in any other developed country. It is projected to rise another 15 per cent in the next 10 years.

The Silver Lining

And the good news? It's saving taxpayers money.

Although healthcare spending for obese people is at least 25 per cent higher than for someone of normal weight, and increases rapidly as people get fatter, severely obese people are likely to die eight to 10 years earlier, so their shorter lives mean they incur lower healthcare costs over their lifetime. It's even greater than the saving on smokers.

If you don't like that, try this. As measured by gross domestic product, obesity is a win-win-win situation. The more you eat the more you add to GDP [gross domestic product] and the profits of businesses. If the messages of advertising and marketing make you self-conscious about your overweight, everything you spend on fancy diets, gym subscriptions etc. adds to GDP.

And then when you damage your health, everything you, the government and your health fund spend on trying to keep you going adds to GDP. Even when you die prematurely that won't count as a negative against GDP, although the absence of your continued consumption will be missed.

Get the feeling there's something amiss?

A Result of Modern Life

Two of our greatest campaigners on obesity are Garry Egger, the professor of lifestyle medicine at Southern Cross University and the founder of GutBusters, and Boyd Swinburn, professor of population health at Deakin University.

They've written a book, *Planet Obesity*, which takes a rather different tack. Since obesity is endemic, it can't be dismissed as the product of gluttony and sloth on the part of a few individuals.

We're getting fatter for a host of interacting reasons.

Obesity has been rising since the 1980s. Before then it was rare. Clearly, it's a product of our modern lifestyle, of the way we organize our society.

We're getting fatter for a host of interacting reasons. According to the OECD report, the supply and availability of food altered remarkably in the second half of the 20th century, brought about by big changes in food production technologies and an increasing and increasingly sophisticated use of promotion and persuasion.

Obesity Rates Among Australian Children

For children and adolescents, the 2007–08 National Health Survey results indicate that 24.9% of children aged 5–17 years are overweight or obese. 25.8% of boys and 24.0% of girls are either overweight or obese.

These results are similar to the 2007 Australian National Children's Nutrition and Physical Activity Survey (the Children's Survey) released in October 2008. The Children's Survey measured food intake, physical activity participation and physical measurements in a sample of 4,487 children aged 2–16 years from across Australia.

Department of Health and Aging,
"Overweight and Obesity in Australia," 2010.

The price of calories fell dramatically and convenience foods became available virtually everywhere, while the time available for traditional meal preparation from raw ingredients shrank as a result of changing working and living conditions.

"Decreased physical activity at work, increased participation of women in the labour force, increasing levels of stress and job insecurity, longer working hours for some jobs, are all factors that, directly or indirectly, contribute to the lifestyle changes which caused the obesity epidemic," the report says.

The Fruits of Our Own Success

See what this is saying? The rise in obesity is a product of the success of capitalism and the technological advance it fosters and exploits.

So far, those who haven't tried to blame the problem on the weakness of individuals have treated it as an unfortunate by-product of modern life, needing to be remedied in some way so we can carry on as usual.

Egger and Swinburn see it very differently, not as a disease but as a signal. "It's the canary in the coal mine, which should alert us to bigger structural problems in society," they say.

The rise in obesity is a product of the success of capitalism and the technological advance it fosters and exploits.

Obesity and the health problems it often brings—type 2 diabetes, heart disease—are part of a rise in chronic conditions, including respiratory disease and many forms of cancer, that could eventually end our ever-increasing longevity, or at least make our longer lives far less pleasant.

People in developed countries have been getting taller and heavier since 1800. For almost all that time, our weight gain has made us healthier but in recent decades it's greatly accelerated and is now making us unhealthy.

The Sweet Spot

So what's the signal Egger and Swinburn say the obesity epidemic is sending us? That we've passed the "sweet spot"—the point where everything's fine, the point of equilibrium, as an economist would say.

Until fairly recently, economic growth was making us unambiguously better off. Making us more secure, more prosperous and, because of scientific advances, improving our health. But now we've overshot the sweet spot and continued economic growth is starting to worsen our health.

It's a similar story with global warming. Economic growth and rising affluence—much of it based on the burning of fossil fuels—was fine as long as the world's sinks could absorb all the extra carbon dioxide we were pumping into the atmosphere.

But now we've passed that point, partly because we've been cutting down and clearing forests and other sinks, greenhouse gases have built up and are adversely affecting the climate. Should we fail to reverse this trend, much worse lies in store.

Finding a Balance

Egger and Swinburn say the trouble with humans is their tendency to overshoot by trying to maximise, rather than optimise, good things such as economic growth and plentiful food.

So the question is how long it will take us to recognise the signal that famine has turned to feast and too much feasting is bad for us. But however long it takes us, our trusty GDP meter will continue assuring us we're doing fine.

Australia's Child Obesity Problem Has Been Exaggerated

The Age

The Age is one of Australia's daily newspapers. In the following viewpoint, the reporter examines claims by health professionals that the child obesity problem in Australia and other developed countries has been exaggerated. Officials assert that childhood obesity has actually remained fairly steady over the past decade, but do discern a trend of higher rates of childhood obesity in low-income families. The author cites experts who believe social justice measures, rather than punitive measures such as a junk food tax, are needed.

As you read, consider the following questions:

1. What is the obesity rate in Australian boys, as cited by the author?

2. As stated by the author, what percentage of Australian girls are obese?

3. As described by the author, what happened to Australia's rate of obesity and overweight between 1985 to 1996?

Australia's childhood obesity problem is an "exaggeration" and calls for a junk food tax will do little to relieve the poverty that is its major driver, an expert says.

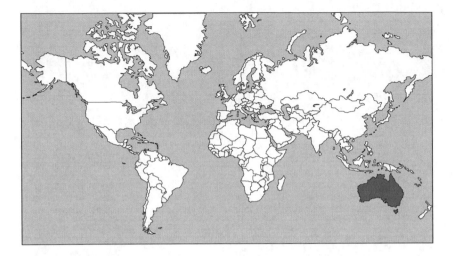

The rate of childhood obesity among low income families was almost double that seen across middle and high income families, said Dr Jennifer O'Dea from the University of Sydney.

She said a tax on junk foods, as called for by a rising number of health experts, would only place extra financial strain on those families when a "social justice" approach was needed.

And while not downplaying the serious health problems that flow from a life of obesity, Dr O'Dea also said the scale of this problem for Australian children has become increasingly overblown.

"People have to stop exaggerating the numbers about childhood obesity—that's not to say that it is not an issue but you know, hysteria, fear campaigns and exaggeration are not very scientific," said Dr O'Dea, who is associate professor in Health Education and Nutrition.

"In children and teenagers, obesity has been stable really since the late 1990s . . . and around Australia, it is still about six per cent."

Childhood obesity rates in Australia, as well as in New Zealand, the US, China and many European countries, have barely budged in the past decade.

Dr O'Dea attributes much of the alarm surrounding the issue today to a sharp rise in childhood obesity in the 1980s and '90s, which was forecast to continue but had not materialised.

In Australia, for example, just one per cent of boys and 0.8 per cent of girls were obese in 1985 and this increased to 5.4 per cent and 5.7 per cent respectively in 1996.

More than a decade later, in 2008, obesity in Australian children was found to be 5.3 per cent for boys—a slight decrease—and 5.9 per cent for girls.

"Because childhood obesity increased in the 1980s doesn't mean that it will continue, and in fact it hasn't," Dr O'Dea said, noting the childhood obesity rate appeared to have "leveled off" and a new balance had been reached.

An obese person is generally considered to have a body mass index (BMI) calculation of 30 or above.

Taking in those children near but not at this level, Australia's rate of overweight and obesity roughly doubled from 1985 to 1996 (from about 11 per cent to 23 per cent) but there was almost no movement to 2008 (24 per cent).

These and other figures are contained in a new book, *Childhood Obesity Prevention*, a collection of international research on the issue and co-edited by Dr O'Dea with Michael Eriksen.

Dr O'Dea said while the evidence pointed to a plateau, it should be noted the data was not as clear-cut as it seemed.

Children went through periods of rapid growth, and those with more advanced muscle development could be deemed to be overweight.

This often included children from a Pacific Islander or Maori background and Dr O'Dea said for many kids "overweight" was not the same as "unfitness".

"Our children have got taller for generations . . . our multicultural society in Australia is going to produce lots of children that are different and diverse," Dr O'Dea said.

"That's something that I think everyone needs to understand."

Dr O'Dea said there was one clear trend, of childhood weight problems concentrated at the lower end of the socioeconomic scale.

She points to her research in 2000 that, in a nationwide study of nearly 5,000 children and teens, found nine per cent of lower socioeconomic status children were obese compared to only five per cent of children from middle or higher income families.

Children went through periods of rapid growth, and those with more advanced muscle development could be deemed to be overweight.

"It's really an issue of social class," Dr O'Dea said.

"And that's where we need to be very careful to approach it as a social justice issue for these low income communities, and disadvantaged communities, where we see the most childhood obesity."

Serving healthy breakfasts in schools—known to stabilise and improve a child's eating pattern throughout the day—was one key way to address the problem, Dr O'Dea said.

She also called for more of a focus on "assisting physical activity in safe neighbourhoods, in school programs, in after-school programs, in noncompetitive physical activity where children can be encouraged to play".

". . . rather than hitting these already disadvantaged parents over the head with a very big stick.

"We have to avoid this blaming and shaming and finger-pointing and focusing on how the parents have failed," Dr O'Dea said.

"I've been very worried that approach will really take hold, and the tax on junk foods is a classic example of that."

Mexico Has a Skyrocketing Obesity Epidemic

Ioan Grillo

Ioan Grillo is a correspondent for Time *magazine. In the following viewpoint, he observes that Mexico has an exploding obesity problem because of a shift from traditional diets to ones rife with processed and fast foods. Grillo argues that much of the problem can be attributed to globalization, which has paved the way for a number of unhealthy food choices.*

As you read, consider the following questions:

1. According to the author, what percentage of Mexican adults are obese?
2. What percentage of Mexican children are overweight, as cited in the viewpoint?
3. As noted in the viewpoint, what product does Mexico consume more of than any other country?

D ressed in the handwoven red cloths of her native village and chatting away in her ancient Nahuatl tongue, Pilar Blanco and her family sit down to dinner in what looks like an age-old mealtime ceremony.

But when Hernandez serves up the food, there is one major difference from tradition: instead of tortillas and beans, the family eats instant noodle soups, potato chips and fizzy soda.

Ioan Grillo, "Mexico's Growing Obesity Problem," GlobalPost, August 29, 2009. Reproduced by permission.

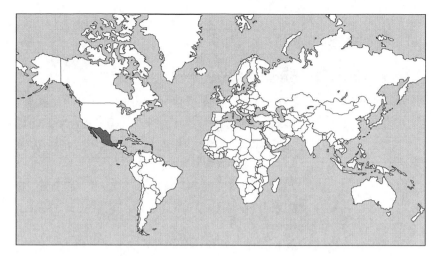

"I'm out working all day cleaning people's houses and I have no time to cook. So the instant soups are a big help," Hernandez explains, sitting with her husband and three children in a cinder block home on the outskirts of this sprawling capital.

The Effects of the Fast-Food Diet

Such radical changes in diet have swept through Mexico in the last decade leading to an explosion of obesity. As families guzzle ever more processed food, hamburgers and French fries, they have piled on the pounds to make Mexico one of fattest nations on the planet.

> *As families guzzle ever more processed food, hamburgers and French fries, they have piled on the pounds to make Mexico one of fattest nations on the planet.*

Studies by the Health Department show that a startling 68 percent of Mexican adults are overweight and 29 percent are obese—just behind the United States, where 74 percent are overweight and 39 percent obese.

Only the tiny Pacific island nations of Samoa and Tonga have heavier populations.

Addressing Childhood Obesity

There is particular concern about the rising weight of Mexican children. The Mexico City government announced this month [August 2009] that an alarming 35 percent of school pupils are over the recommended body weight.

To try to fight back, the government has kick-started an antiobesity campaign of sporting events and healthy-eating propaganda aimed at the young.

"We need you children to understand the importance of taking care of your health and the problem of obesity that is worrying to our country," Mexico City Health Minister Armando Ahued told 1,000 children panting away in a running race. "You are the future of the capital, and we need you to avoid getting diseases such as diabetes and hypertension."

The campaign is also encouraging young people to lose pounds by joining 11,000 dancers in the largest-ever routine of Michael Jackson's song "Thriller," scheduled for Aug. 29 [2009] in Mexico City's central plaza.

Globalization and Food Habits

The changing dietary habits have come as Mexico has switched from a largely protectionist to an extremely globalized economy.

Since it enacted the North American Free Trade Agreement [NAFTA] in 1994, imports of processed food and drinks have soared.

The nation now consumes more Coca-Cola products per capita than anywhere else in the world: a total of 635 eight-ounce bottles per person each year. The amount represents a threefold increase compared to 1988.

In many villages in Mexico's mountains and jungles, it is easier to get a bottle of soda than drinkable water.

Availability of Junk Food Has Increased in Mexico

Along with the decline in physical activity, Mexicans are undergoing a wholesale transformation in eating habits. Besides the imported fast foods, there is an infinite variety of homegrown junk food. Although street stands still sell fresh fruit and juices, corner stores dispense endless cookies, snacks, potato chips and candy.

Elisabeth Malkin,
"Mexico Confronts Sudden Surge in Obesity,"
New York Times, June 29, 2005.

In addition to fattier diets, changing lifestyles have also made people put on the pounds.

More and more Mexicans are abandoning hard-working country jobs for ever expanding urban jungles such as the capital with its 20 million inhabitants or Tijuana, which grows by a block a day.

There are also more and more cars. The country's denizens collectively buy more than a million vehicles a year amid cheaper prices and better credit.

Furthermore, a wave of violent crime makes many parents keep their children at home under their careful eye rather than letting them play on the mean streets.

Policemen themselves have also suffered from the obesity epidemic, undermining their efforts to make these streets safe again. This month, the Public Safety Department called on police to drink more water, eat more healthily and do more exercise to project a better image. The department also sent in a force of 53 experts to train officers to lose weight and engage in sports such as boxing.

Cost to the Health System

As in the United States, Mexico's growing waistline has put immense pressure on the nation's health care system.

Obesity-related diseases cost countless billions in medical attention and lost work hours.

Health officials are particularly concerned about diabetes, with studies showing that Mexicans' genes make them particularly prone to the condition.

"The vulnerability to diabetes comes from both the Indian and Spanish heritage so we are doomed in this sense," said Amanda Galvez, an investigator at Mexico's National Autonomous University. "If we keep eating the way we are eating and if we don't exercise we will all end up having diabetes."

Galvez warns that the worst pressures on the health care system could still be to come.

Many people who have suffered from the obesity epidemic are just reaching middle or old age when they are more prone to crippling diseases.

Manuel Uribe's Achievement

Mexico's most high-profile obesity case entered the Guinness book of records when he went on television to weigh in at 1,235 pounds in 2006.

Since then, Manuel Uribe followed a special diet to drop to 800 pounds.

The 400-pound loss is one of the biggest weight reductions in medical history.

"If I can do it, then others can too," Uribe told reporters as he celebrated the achievement with a band of mariachis last year.

The Mexican government hopes more of its citizens will make such efforts.

South Africa Has a High Rate of Obesity

Belinda Beresford

Belinda Beresford is a writer for the Mail & Guardian. *In the following viewpoint, she maintains that South Africa is struggling with diseases associated with developing countries, such as tuberculosis and HIV, as well as those that usually affect developed countries, such as obesity and associated heart-related conditions. Beresford finds that obesity is such a growing problem in South Africa that it is having serious health and economic effects.*

As you read, consider the following questions:

1. As cited in the viewpoint, what percentage of black women in South Africa are overweight or obese?
2. What percentage of all South Africans over the age of fifteen were overweight or obese, according to a World Health Organization survey in 1998?
3. According to Dr. Martin Mpe, how many South Africans die daily from heart-related issues?

Almost half of adult South Africans are too fat. The health risks are huge: heart-related illness, often triggered by obesity, is the second-biggest killer in the country.

Black women are the most susceptible to health-defying weight problems, closely followed by white men. But fat cuts

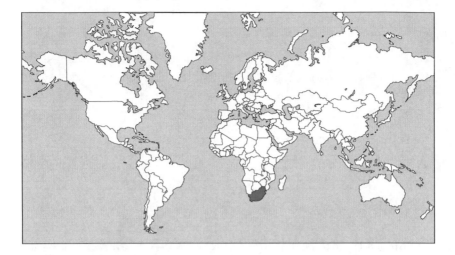

across all social classes. Our children are getting bigger too—thanks to increasingly sedentary lifestyles—and the nation's police force is not entirely fighting fit.

We are a fat nation, and getting fatter as we get richer, take less exercise and gain greater access to fast and ready-made meals.

Simultaneously South Africa is struggling with the classic diseases of a developing country—above all the ugly sisters of HIV and tuberculosis. But the infectious diseases get attention, distracting from the chronic lifestyle-related illnesses more often associated with developed nations such as diabetes, hypertension, cardiovascular disease and high cholesterol levels.

We are a fat nation, and getting fatter as we get richer, take less exercise and gain greater access to fast and ready-made meals.

Gary Fetter, a Johannesburg doctor specialising in the surgical treatment of obesity, says that overweight and obesity are problems affecting all socioeconomic and race groups in South

Africa. But the levels of fatness in this country do vary by gender and race. The most affected group is women—approximately 75% of black women, 42% of white women and 37% of Asian women are estimated to be overweight or obese. Among men, whites are most likely to be overweight or obese at 56%, followed by black men at 49% and then Asian men at 35%.

By the World Health Organization's reckoning in 1998, 45% of all South Africans over the age of 15 were overweight or obese. Most medical professionals agree anecdotally this 10-year-old figure has almost certainly increased. The most common assessment of fatness or thinness is the Body Mass Index (BMI), a single figure calculated using an individual's weight and height.

Overweight is a BMI of between 25 and 30, obese is greater than 30, and morbidly obese is over 40. The BMI as a stand-alone figure is useful, but not always reflective of how healthy or fat a person is. A fit, muscular person may have a high BMI because muscle weighs more than fat. Conversely, a couch potato with very little muscle could have a deceptively low BMI for the same reason.

Even for people with more natural padding against the winter cold, the distribution of fat plays a role. While an apple a day is said to keep the doctor away, an apple-shaped figure may instead lead to more frequent visits to the doctor and possibly an early grave. Far healthier is the stereotyped curvaceous female: big bum and hips, small waist. A waist of more than 80cm for a woman or 94cm for a man is a danger sign, especially if combined with a high BMI.

Fatness carries with it a multitude of health problems: diabetes, hypertension, heightened cholesterol and other fats, increased risk of heart attacks and strokes, bad circulation, leg cramps, impotence—the list goes on.

South Africa Needs to Confront Its Obesity Problem

It is essential that the full range of factors implicated in the pathogenesis and development of obesity, from both an individual and a population perspective, should be fully investigated. In particular, the identification of genes and mutations responsible for the susceptibility to the development of co-morbid diseases and the relative importance of vulnerable periods of life for the development of obesity should be highly prioritised. In South Africa, obesity management programmes should be established within healthcare and community services. Primary healthcare services should play a dominant role in identification of high-risk patients, but hospital and specialist services will be required to deal with complicated patients and to provide optimal treatment of the co-morbid diseases.

H. Salome Kruger et al., "Obesity in South Africa:
Challenges for Government and Health Professionals,"
Public Health Nutrition, *2005.*

Dr Martin Mpe, a Pretoria cardiologist, says almost 200 South Africans die daily from heart-related issues. It is the second-biggest cause of death in South Africa after HIV-related illnesses.

Hypertension—defined as a blood pressure of 140/90mmHG—causes no side effects in 99% of its victims, said Mpe. This makes it particularly dangerous. "You feel nothing until the day you drop dead."

Medication to combat high blood pressure, diabetes and the other problems at least partially associated with being overweight is a thriving business worldwide. But, as Mpe puts it: "The main doctor is the one walking into the doctor's rooms." In other words, prevention or management of the illness is in the patient's own hands.

Obesity leads to high blood pressure and expansion of the heart, damaging other organs and causing arteries to harden and scar. An increase in fat also increases resistance to insulin, leading to type II diabetes. A combination of high blood pressure and diabetes gives an exponential, not an additive risk of early death, says Mpe: a dangerous cocktail of illnesses where the risk of death multiplies.

The financial implications of being overweight from a healthcare perspective are shown by the enthusiasm by some employers and medical schemes to encourage members to move to a healthier—read thinner—lifestyle. Discovery Health, for example, has a wellness programme that encourages members to exercise and eat healthily with incentives such as offering discounts on fresh vegetables at a major supermarket chain.

Losing weight requires a combination of less incoming energy with more outgoing energy—less food and more exercise. Burning 2500 kcal (kilocalories) a week in exercise should drop your risk of early death by 43%. Exercising, even just walking, increases blood flow through the body, opening up blood vessels and leading to a decrease in blood pressure.

Africa Is Affected by Both Hunger and Obesity

IRIN

IRIN is a news agency that focuses on humanitarian issues. In the following viewpoint, the reporter discusses the challenges faced by African countries as they struggle with the effects of both high rates of undernutrition and obesity. In recent years, obesity has been on the rise in African countries as citizens lead more sedentary lives in urban environments and turn to processed and fast foods instead of more traditional diets.

As you read, consider the following questions:

1. What percentage of the world's hungry people live in sub-Saharan Africa, as cited by the author?
2. As noted by the author, what is the rate of overweight and obese women in Africa as of 2004?
3. According to the author, what percentage of Moroccan children were overweight in 2004?

A frica faces a double burden of obesity and hunger as millions take up increasingly sedentary lives in cities and the global financial crisis hits rural populations' food security, nutritionists warn.

Undernutrition continues to plague sub-Saharan Africa, where 32 percent of the world's hungry people live. However,

"Africa: Fighting the 'Double Whammy' of Obesity and Hunger," IRIN, October 8, 2009. Reproduced by permission.

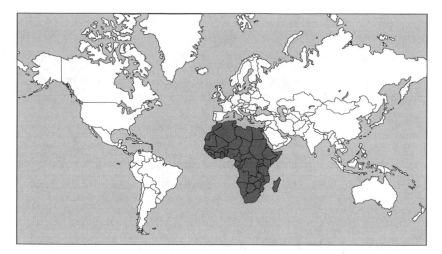

those migrating from the countryside to cities are eating too much fatty food, leading to rising rates of obesity, diabetes, hypertension and high blood pressure, delegates at the International Congress of Nutrition (ICN) in Bangkok were told.

"The problem in Africa is [that] both under and overnutrition are the worst in the world. We really are facing a double burden," Hester Vorster, of the Centre of Excellence in Nutrition at South Africa's North-West University, told the congress, which runs until 9 October [2009].

"Overnutrition is much the same thing as what we see in the West. Significant numbers of Africans have migrated to the cities and they are eating the wrong foods. So for Africa, the burden of disease is increasing all the time," Jean-Claude Mbanya of the University of Yaoundé in Cameroon, and president-elect of the Belgium-based International Diabetes Federation, said.

Poverty and Food Insecurity

Both over and undernutrition can be caused by poverty and food insecurity, with the urban poor unable to access or afford fresh and nutritious food, Helene Delisle, a nutritionist at the University of Montreal in Canada, told IRIN.

In some northern and southern African countries, overnutrition has surpassed undernutrition, but there is a complete lack of awareness about the new problems it brings, she said.

"These countries are not aware of it. In many areas, obesity is seen not as a problem, but as a positive sign that you are doing well in life," she said.

Meanwhile, lower-income countries continue to suffer mainly from undernutrition, which has actually increased over the past five years, thanks to the food price crisis of 2008 and the global financial crisis, Delisle said.

Obesity on the Rise

Statistics from the World Health Organization (WHO) show how obesity has risen while undernutrition has persisted in some countries.

In Madagascar in 1992, just 1.6 percent of children were overweight, while 35.5 percent were underweight and 60.9 percent suffered stunted growth. By 2004, 6.2 percent of children were overweight while 36.8 percent were underweight, and 52.8 percent were stunted.

The rate of overweight and obese women also doubled between 1997 and 2004, to 8.1 percent overall.

Statistics from the World Health Organization (WHO) show how obesity has risen while undernutrition has persisted in some countries.

And in 1987, 5.5 percent of Moroccan children were overweight; by 2004, that figure had increased to 13.3 percent.

Obesity is also on the rise in Uganda, although undernutrition continues to pose the biggest problem, with about 40 percent of children under five suffering from stunted physical growth and mental development due to a lack of vitamins and nutrient-rich food.

Obesity and other so-called "lifestyle diseases" are widely regarded as a problem only for older people in Uganda but are increasingly prevalent in young men, Elizabeth Madraa, the head of food and nutrition at Uganda's Ministry of Health, and a delegate at the congress, told IRIN.

Anaemia in teenage girls is also increasing due to a lack of iron in diets, she said. And in another new trend, Ugandan mothers are increasingly choosing to give their babies powdered milk rather than breastfeeding them.

"They buy milk powder because they see it advertised, and we have to fight that. We need to address all this as a nutrition problem," Madraa said.

Greater Awareness

Mbanya called for awareness campaigns and legislation to fight the negative effects of a poor diet fuelled partly by advertising. "If we want our people to change their habits we have to make it easy for them to have healthy choices," he said.

However, progress is hampered by the poor status of nutritional science in Africa, experts say.

Few well-defined job openings, poor salaries and recognition, and a plethora of competing curricula taught by unqualified trainers are among the challenges, said Tola Atinmo, Nigerian president of the Federation of African Nutrition Societies.

"At the moment in Africa, nutrition is everybody's problem but nobody's business," said Atinmo.

Obesity Is Virtually Nonexistent in Japan

Erica Angyal

Erica Angyal is a nutritionist, health specialist, and author. In the following viewpoint, she examines the reasons why Japan does not have an obesity problem, citing the country's traditional diet, genetics, and cultural pressures. Angyal surveys the findings of a recent best seller by Naomi Moriyama that finds that Americans consume too many calories, serve too-large portions of food, and eat too much processed and fast foods compared to the Japanese. Angyal makes note of other issues, though, such as increased consumption of fast food and the prevalence of eating disorders.

As you read, consider the following questions:

1. According to the author, what is the obesity rate for women in Japan?
2. How many calories per day do Japanese people eat typically, as outlined by the author?
3. According to the author, how many calories per day does an average American eat?

Who has the global bragging rights to slimness? First there was Mireille Guiliano's book, *French Women Don't Get Fat: The Secret of Eating for Pleasure*, published in 2004.

Erica Angyal, "How Japan Became No. 1," *Japan Times*, February 7, 2006. Reproduced by permission.

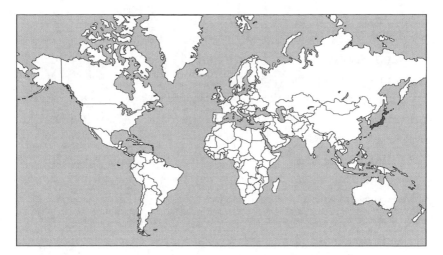

Hot on the heels of this best seller, Naomi Moriyama threw down the gauntlet less than a year later with *Japanese Women Don't Get Old or Fat: Secrets of My Mother's Tokyo Kitchen*—taking it one step further by adding longevity to the equation.

For those who travel to places like the United States, Europe or Australia, it is often a great shock to see how many people are overweight or outright obese, but how few plus sizes we encounter when walking the streets of Japan. According to the latest figures from the International Obesity Task-Force and the World Health Organization (WHO), Japanese women have the lowest obesity rate in the industrialized world—a tiny 3 percent, compared with 11 percent in France and a whopping 34 percent in the United States. Japanese women also enjoy the world's highest life expectancy—85 years. (It's a close race though: Italian and French women are just behind at 84 years and Swedish, Swiss and Australian women are on 83 years).

The Advantage of a Japanese Diet

The virtually nonexistent rates of obesity in Japan are intriguing when you consider how food obsessed the country really is, with more cooking programs and gourmet magazines than you can throw a breadstick at. Part of the explanation, says Moriyama, lies inside the nutritional value of Japanese cooking, and in the kind of food prepared by her mother and millions of other Japanese mothers.

A marketing consultant who was born in Tokyo but currently resides in New York with her husband and coauthor, William Doyle, Moriyama says that it's not just genetics that keep the Japanese so enviably trim. While she was a college student in the U.S, she packed on 12 kg [kilograms] and not long after she returned home after two years, the extra weight fell off naturally. She attributed the loss to her mother's home-cooked food.

> *The virtually nonexistent rates of obesity in Japan are intriguing when you consider how food obsessed the country really is, with more cooking programs and gourmet magazines than you can throw a breadstick at.*

"I live in New York and I grew up in Tokyo eating my mom's good old-fashioned traditional Japanese home cooking. Every time my American husband and I went back to eat at my mother's Tokyo kitchen, we would lose weight and feel fantastic. We wrote this book to explore why this was happening."

According to Moriyama, who is 45, the "secret" of staying svelte is simply to eat a traditional Japanese diet comprising fish, vegetables, fruit, rice and soy.

The Japanese Kitchen

Moriyama believes a difference in the grocery-shopping habits play a part, too. "On average, Japanese women are buying more fish, rice, soy and fresh vegetables—and smaller amounts of less healthy foods like red meat, candy, cookies, potato chips, pastries and processed foods," she says. "Japanese have smaller kitchens and less storage than Americans, so they have to go to the supermarket more often to shop for fresh fish, vegetables and fruit. In America, there's more room to store things like frozen and canned foods, and people stock up for weeks at a time. In Japan, there is a cultural preoccupation with buying produce that is *shun* [in season]. That's a health advantage, since nutritionists tell us 'fresh is best' for fruits and vegetables."

When it comes to eating, Moriyama recommends the Japanese saying, "Hara *hachi bunme* (Eat until you are 80 percent full.)" In short, stop short of stuffing yourself.

Difference in Portion Sizes

Portion sizes are, of course, part of the problem. People become accustomed to volume, and to stay in business, restaurants and supermarkets have to cater to that demand.

"In the United States, the size of an average portion has completely exploded over the past few decades, which has helped trigger a rapid rise in obesity, which we're also seeing in Europe and Australia," Moriyama says. "The results of Japanese-style portion control are striking. On average, Japanese people consume 2,700 calories per person per day, compared with 3,700 per person in the U.S. That means Japanese eat 1,000 calories a day less than Americans, even though Japanese are, on average, only about two or three inches shorter than Americans."

People become accustomed to volume, and to stay in business, restaurants and supermarkets have to cater to that demand.

She mentions an anecdote about Japanese sumo wrestlers who toured Las Vegas a few months ago. "One of them looked at an all-you-can-eat buffet table at one of the casinos and marveled to a *Wall Street Journal* reporter, 'Everything is so

---

Why Japan Does Not Have an Obesity Problem

- Japanese eat more fat, and therefore less carbs, than Americans

- Japanese chain-drink caffeinated, unsweetened tea, not HFCS [high-fructose corn syrup] soft drinks

- Japanese don't snack to the degree that Americans do

- Japanese walk at least 40 min., 5 times per week

- Japanese walk/ride bikes more often than Americans

Paul Ericson, "Obesity in Japan,"
Liberation Wellness, *March 6, 2010.*

---

big here. It makes me feel small.' Another one stared at a jumbo pastrami sandwich and said, 'It's too big.' These are sumo wrestlers!"

A Zen Approach

Moriyama suggests taking a Zen approach to food: "Choose the freshest ingredients, cook gently, serve more fish, rice, fresh fruit and vegetables, and take time to slow down and eat with your eyes as well as your mouth—savor and admire the natural beauty and flavor of your food. The secret to enjoying food is to fully appreciate how beautiful it is. Beautiful presentation is the lifeblood of Japanese cuisine."

To non-Japanese cooks, she gives the following tip: "Give your regular big dishes and plates a vacation—try serving more modest portions on the small salad and appetizer dishes you already have in your cupboard. Don't think of it as portion control; think of it as portion liberation."

The Benefits of a Traditional Diet

While much of the wisdom contained in *Japanese Women Don't Get Old or Fat* might not be breaking news on these shores, the book is a valuable reminder of the inherent health benefits of a traditional diet. To research the book, Moriyama and Doyle interviewed over 30 top science and medicine experts on the subjects of longevity, health and nutrition. "They attribute Japanese longevity to a number of factors—diet and lifestyle; strong social and spiritual ties; a sophisticated health-care system, perhaps some genetic advantages, and 'incidental exercise'—the fact that Japanese are more likely to walk or ride bikes in their daily lives than many Westerners.

As Moriyama's book has been embraced enthusiastically in the U.S., as well as Britain and Australia (where it's subtitled "Delicious Slimming and Anti-Ageing Secrets" and published by Vermillion), she certainly seems to have tapped into the zeitgeist of going back to more traditional ways. However, when you take a closer look at the reality of everyday Japan, a number of disturbing trends are emerging. The awful truth is that many Japanese love their fast food, be it Yoshinoya beef bowls or Big Macs, and breakfast these days is more likely to be white toast and a coffee than miso soup and grilled fish.

Cultural Pressures

Also, there seems to be something else at work: an obsession with being thin. Japan has the highest rates of anorexia and bulimia in the world, and Moriyama notes there is indeed an enormous social pressure to be thin in Japan. For many young women, dieting is a way of life. This desire to be thin may explain the drop in BMI (Body Mass Index) in younger women. BMI equals a person's weight divided by his or her height in meters squared. The problem of "extreme thinness" among Japanese women (which is classified here as being below 17 kg/m2 grew from 2.4 percent in 1976–1980 to 4.2 percent in 1996–2000 among young women (ages 15–29 years). The drop in BMI among young and early-middle-age Japanese women is most noticeable in metropolitan areas such as Tokyo.

A Coming Crisis?

Yet Moriyama also admits there is an obesity crisis on the horizon in Japan, especially among certain segments of children and middle-aged men. What's more, the increased weight among Japanese men and older women is not always represented by the BMI because when they gain weight, it tends to accumulate in the abdominal region and not the legs and arms. This is the worst place to gain weight as it is more closely tied to increases in chronic disease, such as cardiovascular disease and diabetes. The Japanese waist circumference is increasing, and adults who are not technically even overweight according to the BMI, let alone obese, are showing increased waist circumference.

What's interesting is that women in neighboring South Korea also boast an obesity rate of only 3 percent. So perhaps the next book to emerge from a marketing executive will be *Why Korean Women Don't Get Fat*, expounding the benefits of *kimchi* (a traditional Korean dish of fermented chili peppers and cabbage) and *yakiniku* (Korean barbecue chicken) with sunny lettuce.

Moriyama acknowledges that the traditional Japanese diet isn't perfect and that it's often far too high in sodium, from salty foods like pickled vegetables, soy sauce and miso soup.

While the national diet has definite virtues, Moriyama believes that Japan is at a crossroads: "If it chooses the path of too much fast food, Western-sized portions and less physical activity, it may become a fat nation with an out-of-control obesity epidemic in 10 years or so. But if it holds onto its roots in the traditional Japanese diet and lifestyle, it can continue as the world's healthiest nation."

We hope it chooses the latter.

Periodical and Internet Sources Bibliography

The following articles have been selected to supplement the diverse views presented in this chapter.

Dudley Althaus "Obesity Up in Mexico, Especially Among Kids," *Houston Chronicle*, January 28, 2010.

BBC News "Obesity Affects One in 10 Adults Around the World," February 3, 2011. www.bbc.co.uk.

Jay Bhattacharya "Dollars to Doughnuts," *Hoover Digest*, June 19, 2007.

Zoi Constantine "Middle East Suffering from Obesity and Under-Nutrition at Same Time, Conference Is Told," *National*, May 26, 2010.

FoxNews.com "Global Obesity Rates Have Doubled Since 1980: Study Says," February 4, 2011. www.fox news.com.

Sander L. Gilman "Fat Chance," Project Syndicate, September 30, 2009. www.project-syndicate.org.

Jonathan Hiskes "Globesity: How Climate Change and Obesity Draw from the Same Roots," Grist.org, June 12, 2009. www.grist.org.

Calum MacLeod "Obesity of China's Kids Stuns Officials," *USA Today*, January 9, 2007.

Franco Ordonez "Mexico Is Second-Fattest Nation After U.S.," *San Diego Union-Tribune*, March 24, 2008.

André Picard "Growth of Obesity in Poor Countries Alarming: Researchers," *Globe & Mail*, February 3, 2011.

Carly Weeks "U.S.-Canadian Obesity Gap Is Narrowing," *Globe & Mail*, March 2, 2011.

GLOBALVIEWPOINTS

CHAPTER 2

Obesity Factors

Mauritanian Culture Encourages Women to Be Obese

Kuwait Times

The Kuwait Times *is an English-language daily newspaper published in Kuwait. In the following viewpoint, the reporter chronicles the persisting beauty ideal in the African nation of Mauritania for obese women, observing that it has resulted in a variety of weight-related health problems for women in that country who are often force-fed to gain weight. The reporter notes that this ideal endures despite the government's growing efforts to counteract it by showing images of slimmer body types and promoting safe and healthy eating practices.*

As you read, consider the following questions:

1. What is the tradition of "gavage," as explained in the viewpoint?
2. According to the viewpoint, how many women in Mauritania under the age of nineteen have been force-fed?
3. As explained by the author, what percentage of women over thirty in Saudi Arabia are obese?

S he struggles under her own weight, lumbering up the stairs, her thighs shaking with each step. Once she reaches the top, it will take several minutes for 50-year-old Mey Mint to

"'Fat Is Beautiful' View of Women Still Persists," *Kuwait Times*, April 18, 2007. Reproduced by permission.

catch her breath, the air hissing painfully in and out of her chest. Her rippling flesh is not the result of careless overeating, but rather of a tradition of force-feeding girls in a desert nation where obesity has long been the ideal of beauty, signalling a family's wealth in a land repeatedly wracked by drought.

To make a girl big and plump, the tradition of 'gavage'—a French word borrowed from the practice of fattening of geese for foie gras—starts as early as 4, as it did for Mint, who was forced to drink 55 litres of camel's milk a day. When she vomited, she was beaten. If she refused to drink, her fingers were bent back until they touched her hand. Her stomach hurt so much she prayed all the animals in the world would die so that there would be no more milk to be had.

Now, she has trouble walking and suffers from a combination of weight-related illnesses, including diabetes and heart disease. "My mother thinks she made me beautiful. But she made me sick," says Mint, who asked that her full last name not be disclosed because she feels embarrassed by her past. To end the brutal practice, the government launched a TV and radio campaign highlighting the risks of obesity. Because most Mauritanian love songs describe the ideal woman as fat, the Health Ministry commissioned catchy odes to thin women.

Anti-Obesity Efforts

These efforts, combined with the rising popularity of foreign soap operas featuring model-thin women, has helped stamp out the practice among the country's urban elite. Only one in 10 women under age 19 has been force-fed, compared to a third of women 40 or older, according to a survey by the National Statistics Office in 2001, the most recent available. Those who were forced to eat were overwhelmingly from the country's rural areas. But although the canon of beauty is changing, entrenched values are hard to uproot.

"My husband thinks I'm not fat enough," complained Zeinabou Mint Bilkhere, explaining that her husband found her pretty during the last months of her pregnancy. Since giving birth, the weight has dropped, however, and with it his desire for her. Although force-feeding has decreased, many women feel pressured to be bigger than average and have turned to a more scientific method of weight gain, using foreign-made, appetite-inducing pills.

Although force-feeding has decreased, many women feel pressured to be bigger than average and have turned to a more scientific method of weight gain, using foreign-made, appetite-inducing pills.

Wrapped in a floor-length veil, the 24-year-old who is roughly a size 8, opens her purse and pushes a fistful of change across the counter of a roadside pharmacy in exchange for a box of Anactine, a Moroccan-made antihistamine. The pills, commonly prescribed for hay fever, have as their side effect an unabated desire to eat. A variety of appetite boosters are popular in Mauritania, including antihistamines made by the likes of Merck and Novartis. They replace a more blunt instrument, recently outlawed by the government—animal steroids intended for fattening camels.

The Mauritania Beauty Ideal

For decades, the Mauritanian version of a Western teenager's crash diet was a crash feeding program, devised to create girls obese enough to display family wealth and epitomize the Mauritanian ideal. Centuries-old poems glorified women immobilized by fat, moving so slowly they seemed to stand still, unable to hoist themselves onto camels without the aid of men's willing hands.

Sharon LaFraniere,
"In Mauritania, Seeking to End an Overfed Ideal,"
New York Times, *July 4, 2007.*

Cultural Pressures

"When I was little my mother hit me to eat because I didn't want to be fat. Now I want to be big because men like that," said Bilkhere who hopes the antihistamines will help her gain 10 to 15 kg. A common Moor saying holds that the place a woman occupies in a man's heart is according to her volume. Even as infomercials tout the health benefits of being thin, many men say they prefer voluptuous women.

Isselmou Ould Mohamed says he loves his wife's 90-kg body and was secretly pleased when she began putting on even more weight during pregnancy. When he learned that to shed the extra pounds she was walking around the football stadium in the Mauritanian capital Nouakchott, he was revolted. "I don't like skinny women. I want to be able to grab her love handles," says the 32-year-old. "I told her that if she loses a lot of weight, I'll divorce her." One Internet cafe owner says when he's closing at night, he sometimes finds computer screens left open to porn sites dedicated to XL [extra large] women.

The History of the Tradition

Obesity is a tradition across much of the Arab world, where nomadic peoples struggling to survive the harshness of the desert came to prize fatness as a sign of health. Forty-four percent of women over 30 in Saudi Arabia are obese, as are approximately a third of adult women in Egypt, Bahrain and Kuwait, according to data from the International Obesity Task-Force in London. "A man's goal is to marry a woman that fills his house. She needs to decorate it like an armoire or a TV set. If she's big, she gives the house importance. If she's thin, she disappears," said Seif l'Islam, 48, curator of a library of ancient Islamic manuscripts, including numerous love poems to plump women.

Although the old idea of beauty is far from dead, one sign of change is the recent fitness trend. In the dying desert light, chubby women in head-to-toe veils walk around the capital's dusty football stadium, visibly perspiring in a scene that would have been considered unseemly a decade ago. When she first started walking laps six years ago, 40-year-old Ramla Mint Ahmed said she wrapped her orange veil tightly around her face hoping not to be recognized. Now she exercises openly. She is even on a diet hoping to lose the rings of fat encircling her stomach. Her obese mother, who as a child was awakened in the night and forced to drink camel's milk, says she doesn't object to her daughter dieting.

> *Obesity is a tradition across much of the Arab world, where nomadic peoples struggling to survive the harshness of the desert came to prize fatness as a sign of health.*

That doesn't mean the older woman's notion of beauty has changed. Ahmed is the eldest of three daughters and the only overweight one. Her 22- and 26-year-old sisters are no larger than a size 4 and have long, gazelle-like legs. In America, they would be envied for their tiny waists, yet their mother sees them differently. Asked which of her three daughters is the prettiest, she waves her hand dismissively toward the model-thin sisters, saying, "Definitely those two are not beautiful." Her oldest daughter, like her, has garlands of fat on her belly, voluminous thighs and deep, heaving breasts. "This one," says the mother, "has the face of a queen."

Czech Republic's Obesity Problem Is Linked to Diet and Sedentary Lifestyle

Kimberly Ashton

Kimberly Ashton is a contributor to the Prague Post. *In the following viewpoint, she surveys the growing obesity problem among the citizens of the Czech Republic that has made them among the heaviest Europeans. Ashton notes that the obesity rates are particularly pronounced in suburban and rural areas, which combine a rich traditional Czech diet with a more sedentary lifestyle. To treat the widespread obesity problem, a number of weight-treatment centers have been established across the country.*

As you read, consider the following questions:

1. As stated by the author, where does the Czech Republic usually rank on the list of the heaviest countries in Europe?
2. What percentage of Czech adults are obese, according to the author?
3. According to the author, what percentage of Czech children are overweight?

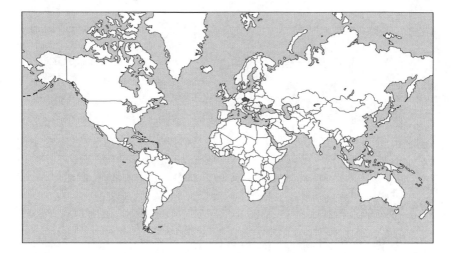

Praguers—especially the women—are known as a preter-naturally, inexplicably svelte group despite the standard Czech diet of dumplings, pork and beer.

But all that heavy food, and changing lifestyles, has caught up with Czechs. Studies now show that they are among the heftiest people on the continent.

Czechs are getting fatter for the same reasons that Americans, and now the British, have notoriously enlarged: They eat too much and do too little.

"The Czech people have a high rate of obesity," said Dr. Vojtch Hainer, of the Czech Institute of Endocrinology in Prague and president of the European Association for the Study of Obesity.

Czechs are getting fatter for the same reasons that Americans, and now the British, have notoriously enlarged: They eat too much and do too little.

Although studies measuring obesity vary in method from country to country, Hainer said Czechs are usually somewhere between the third to fifth heaviest in Europe. The British tend to lead the pack, and Poland, Germany and Cyprus pull more than their own weight, too.

The thinnest nations are Italy and France, according to the International Association for the Study of Obesity. Scandinavians, who Hainer noted bicycle a lot, tend to be slender, too.

Old Habits Die Hard

More than half of Czech adults are overweight, meaning they have a Body Mass Index (BMI) of more than 25; and about 20 percent are obese, meaning they have a BMI of more than 30. A person's BMI is his or her weight divided by the square of the person's height.

It's not an optimum measure of fat stores, just a "very crude mark of overweight and obesity," Hainer said.

For example, men tend to have higher BMI than women because of their lean muscle mass, not necessarily because they have more fat.

Children, too, are getting heavier. Hainer said about 10 percent to 20 percent of Czech children are overweight. The reasons for this increase, for both children and adults, are that the Czech lifestyle is increasingly sedentary and Czechs tend to consume a lot of fats and sugars. High beer consumption also factors. Hainer has said high alcohol consumption is associated with enlarged fat stores.

Especially since the fall of communism, Czechs have had an increasing variety of food to eat—but, for some, old habits die hard.

Philip James, former chairman of the London-based International Obesity TaskForce, said central and eastern Europe rank at the top of middle-aged obesity because Communist-era agricultural and food policies focused on producing and eating meat and fat, according to the *Canadian Medical Association Journal*.

Another Factor in the Czech Republic's Obesity Crisis

[It] is not only food that is causing concern amongst experts [in the Czech Republic]. As the country is famous for its beer production and consumption, drink is also a major part of the average Czech diet. The brewing industry has seen continual growth in recent years, both in domestic consumption and in its exports.

Chris Jarrett,
"Food, Glorious Food—Czech Eating Habits After 1989,"
Radio Prague, March 30, 2006.

The upside of the increased variety is that more people, and especially the young, are eating more fruits and vegetables. The downside is they are also drinking more soda and other sugary drinks and gobbling down snacks, Hainer said. U.S. studies have strongly correlated childhood obesity with the consumption of sugary drinks.

Treatment Necessary

The effect of this combination of sloth and gluttony tends to be particularly pronounced outside of cities.

"[Obesity] is much higher in the countryside because they really combine the traditional Czech food with the sedentary lifestyle," Hainer said.

The young tend to eat less traditionally Czech food, but their sedentary habits mean they are still putting on the kilos.

To fight the nation's expanding waistline, a number of obesity-treatment centers have been established across the country.

Dr. Marie Kunešová, also of the endocrinological institute, told Radio Prague that there are five centers in the Czech Republic for the treatment of severely obese patients and about 40 obesity outpatient clinics. She has said more people driving is also to blame.

Kunešová put the obesity numbers at 22 percent for men and 25 percent for women and said that a dozen years ago the numbers were 16 percent and 20 percent, respectively. The European Association for the Study of Obesity (EASO) expects these numbers will rise, as they have in the United States.

Only in a few European countries—the Czech Republic, Georgia and Serbia—are obese patients directed toward specialists for management and treatment, according to the EASO. Treatment is necessary to prevent obesity-related killers such as hypertension and diabetes.

American Culture Makes the War on Obesity Difficult

George F. Will

George F. Will is an author and syndicated political newspaper columnist. In the following viewpoint, he attributes America's obesity problem to an inability to effectively deal with the freedom and affluence that characterize American life. Will argues that issues of self-control and willpower are problematic in a society rife with choices and temptations, especially when corporations market to those weaknesses and technological advances facilitate bad choices.

As you read, consider the following questions:

1. As noted by Will, what essayist and novelist has written about the problems and affluence of American life?
2. What percentage of Americans are obese, according to Will?
3. According to the viewpoint, how much has Americans' per capital caloric intake increased since 1980?

Wonder why you have already broken all your New Year's resolutions? Do not blame yourself—heaven forbid. Enlist modern sophistication and blame your brain's frontal cortex, affluence, the Internet (the "collapse of delay between impulse and action") and "the democratization of temptation."

George F. Will, "America Is Losing the War on Itself," *National Post*, January 10, 2011. Reproduced by permission.

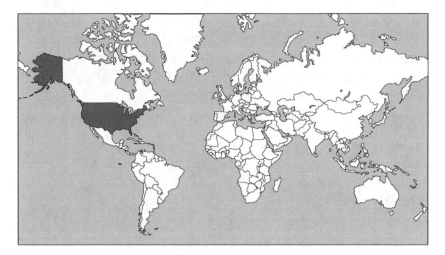

Those phrases are from Daniel Akst, a novelist and essayist whose book *We Have Met the Enemy: Self-Control in an Age of Excess* notes that the problems of freedom and affluence—of "managing desire in a landscape rich with temptation"—are desirable problems. But they are problems and have fascinating philosophic entanglements.

American life resembles "a giant all-you-can-eat buffet" offering "calories, credit, sex, intoxicants" and other invitations to excess. Americans accept these invitations so promiscuously that bad decisions about smoking, eating, drinking and other behaviors account for almost half of U.S. deaths in "our losing war with ourselves."

Life in general has become what alcohol is—disinhibiting. First, America was transformed from a nation of want into one of wants. Then the 1960s repudiated restraint, equating it with repression. Next, inflation in the 1970s discouraged delay of gratification.

The Divided Nature of Modern Life

Today capitalism has a bipolar disorder, demanding self-controlled workers yet uninhibited shoppers. "Want to buy something?" Akst asks. "Chances are that nearby stores are open (many Wal-Marts virtually never close), and with plastic in your pocket you've got the wherewithal." The Internet further reduces life's "frictional costs." But it increases distractions. Increasingly, Americans work at devices that can be stereos, game players, telephones, movie screens and TVs.

The inhibiting intimacy of the village has been supplanted by the city's "disinhibiting anonymity." Even families have dispersed within the home: Time was, they listened to one radio together; then came the transistor. As traditional social structures have withered under disapproval, and personal choice and self-invention have been celebrated, "second careers, second homes, second spouses, and even second childhoods are commonplace."

What the cartoon character Pogo said many decades ago ("We have met the enemy and he is us") is especially true of Americans wielding knives and forks: One-third are merely overweight, another third are obese. Since 1980, obesity has doubled. Akst says 1980 was about the time when the microwave oven became ubiquitous: The oven is emblematic of the plummeting effort required per calorie ingested. One estimate is that Americans' per capita caloric intake has increased 22% since 1980, and the number of diabetics has more than quadrupled.

American life resembles "a giant all-you-can-eat buffet" offering "calories, credit, sex, intoxicants" and other invitations to excess.

The "Aristocracy of Self-Control"

Pondering America's "aristocracy of self-control," Akst notes that affluent people, for whom food is a relatively minor expense, are less likely than poor people to be obese. Surely this has something to do with habits of self-control that are conducive to social success generally.

"Obesity in America," cartoon by Felipe Galindo, www.CartoonStock.com. Copyright © Felipe Galindo. Reproduction rights obtainable from www.CartoonStock.com.

Environmental stimuli and our genetic inheritances circumscribe self-control, but Akst insists that we are not merely fleshy robots responding to them. Skepticism about free will has, however, become convenient and soothing, because exculpatory behaviors once considered signs of bad character have been drained of moral taint by being medicalized as "addictions." When a political operative went five years without filing income tax returns, his lawyer explained this as "non-filer syndrome." Akst wonders: "Isn't it possible we are confusing human diversity with disease?"

If someone holds a gun to your head and demands, "Don't blink or I'll shoot," you are doomed. But not if the demand is "Don't drink or I'll shoot." Unlike Isaac Bashevis Singer, who said, "Of course I believe in free will—I have no choice," Akst sides with William James: "My first act of free will shall be to believe in free will." Akst says "we create the patterns that we are victims of," and he considers the idea of self-control "perhaps tautological" because "who else besides me could possibly be in charge of myself, after all?"

As Akst recognizes, arguments about the reality of personal autonomy have political resonances: "If you believe your life is largely the result of your own discipline and decisions, you're going to feel very differently about taxes, regulations and redistribution than if you believe your life is largely the sum of your genes and your environment—factors irretrievably beyond your control."

Willpower, Akst says, is like a muscle that can be strengthened but is susceptible to exhaustion. Did you tell lots of people—did you blog about—your New Year's resolutions? Akst knows why you didn't: "self-control fatigue," which is as American as microwaved apple pie.

In India, Wealth Increases the Likelihood of Obesity

Nina Martyris

Nina Martyris is a journalist and contributor to the Guardian. *In the following viewpoint, she points out that the problem of obesity is concentrated in the middle class in India, where junk food is affordable to only the well-off. Martyris contrasts this with the obesity problem in the United States that occurs in low-income families.*

As you read, consider the following questions:

1. According to the author, how many children in a Delhi private school are obese?
2. How many schoolchildren in the United States are obese or overweight, as stated by the author?
3. According to Martyris, what percentage of parents and teachers do not think of samosas as junk food?

The Diabetes Foundation (India) has published a study that cuts right to India's bourgeois bone. It says that one in every three schoolchildren in a Delhi private school is obese. Private schools in Mumbai are marginally less plump. Kids are consuming four times the recommended quantity of food.

The study was published barely a week after the evangelist of healthy eating, Michelle Obama, and her husband, President Barack Obama, visited the country. Ever since she launched Let's Move!, her campaign to defeat the epidemic of childhood obesity in the US, Michelle Obama has repeatedly hurled a hefty statistic at her audience to underscore the urgency of the fight against fat: One in every three schoolchildren in the US is obese or overweight; among African-American children it is even higher.

Mirror Images: Obesity in India and the United States

Obama could, perhaps, have talked about the virtues of healthy eating to the orphans and street kids she danced and played hopscotch with in Mumbai. Except that her target audience would have been wrong. India's poor are not the ones battling the bulge. They're still stuck with malnutrition.

In the US it's quite the opposite. Poverty and obesity are joined at the hip in America—strikingly, the 10 poorest and 10 fattest states are almost the same just as prosperity and obesity are bedfellows in India. Obesity may have gone viral in both developing and developed countries but the difference is that the affected groups occupy two opposite ends of the food chain.

The price of foods appears to be the defining factor. It's ironic that while the American poor can only afford to buy junk, in India junk is affordable only to the well-off. Burgers and pastries are beyond the purse of the bulk of the population, who, to put it darkly, are insulated by their poverty in the same way that Burma is insulated from KFC and McDonald's by sanctions.

Factors in Obesity Crisis in India

The causes for body sprawl in both countries are well known. Childhood obesity in India is an urban, post-lib plague fuelled by too much couch, too many snacks and an addiction to apples that are flat, shiny and digital. It doesn't help that the Indian metabolism is predisposed to fat accumulation around the waist. Aggressive fast-food multinationals have localised flavours and chutneyfied their advertising hustle to successfully colonise the Indian gut. Children have a special place in their hearts.

Lifestyles have changed profoundly. Only a generation ago, families ate out sparingly, children walked or cycled to school with a tiffin-box of homemade lunch and a slab of Cadbury's milk chocolate was carefully split by the whole family. Affluence and rapid Westernisation makes all that sound rather quaint. Go check the size of the popcorn tubs at any Mumbai multiplex.

Making the Right Choices

In the US, nutritionists point out that a bucket of fried chicken or free refills of Coke are cynically low in price to subsidise bad eating habits. If the poor had the purchasing power and access to healthy food, runs the argument, they would consume it.

A Genetic Propensity for Obesity?

[Dr. Pradeep] Chowbey fears that Indians may be at greater risk from obesity than Westerners—precisely because of their history of undernourishment. A current theory is that generations of hunger and deprivation have made Indians develop so-called "thrifty genes" that store more fat than those of people who have been well fed. The idea of a genetic propensity to gain weight is a theory that has not yet been conclusively proved, but it is one that has many adherents around the world, including in the US and Britain.

Justin Huggler, "Health vs. Wealth: India's Big Problem,"
Independent, *August 4, 2006.*

The troubling question is: Would they? Eating right and staying fit sounds charming but it requires herculean willpower to wean palates off deep-fried nirvana. Depression, unemployment and homelessness make the fight harder. The appeal of carrot sticks or a chicken-and-lettuce salad wilts rapidly when confronted with a sizzling slice of pizza entombed in mozzarella and pepperoni.

India, with the world's second-largest diabetes population, has not yet woken up to the ticking cholesterol bomb in its midst.

Consumption Illiteracy

Does the fight, then, come down to what is tastier? Why else would the middle class in India, which has access to reasonably priced fruits and vegetables, reach for junk? Because we are consumption illiterate, says Dr Anoop Misra, director of the Diabetes Foundation (India). "We may live in the 21st century and have money, but our thinking is so 19th century, that we have come out of a famine, so we should eat whatever is available without thinking of excess food or processed food. 50% of parents and teachers interviewed didn't think of samosas as junk food. The affluent may now know about olive oil and gyms but the lower middle class and middle class have little awareness. All party food has to be fried—trans fat-engorged samosas, pakoras, bhatura—and while there is nothing new about this, party-throwing has shot up and alcohol is no longer a stigma."

The obesity epidemic in the US has triggered a heated political conversation on the economic impact of related diseases such as diabetes, cancer and cardiac and respiratory problems. India, with the world's second-largest diabetes population, has not yet woken up to the ticking cholesterol bomb in its midst. It's not too late. More critically, a country with the largest number of chronically malnourished children in the world would be ill-served if its stretched resources were diverted to fight a big, fat lifestyle problem.

In Pakistan, Obesity in Students Is Caused by Unhealthy Choices

Rabail Qadeer Baig

Rabail Qadeer Baig is a staff writer for Dawn, *an English-language newspaper in Pakistan. In the following viewpoint, she examines the high obesity rates in Pakistan, maintaining that unhealthy eating habits often develop while students are in college, where many young Pakistani men and women take advantage of the convenience of fast food and gain weight on junk food. Baig suggests that there should be mandatory nutrition classes for all students in order to instruct them on healthy eating habits and to avoid later weight-related health problems.*

As you read, consider the following questions:

1. According to the viewpoint, how many young adults in Pakistan are obese or overweight?

2. How many pounds does the typical college student gain in their freshman year, as noted by the viewpoint?

3. How many people in Pakistan have diabetes, according to the author?

It's amazing how pervasive yet insidious food has become. These days, every second commercial on TV is of some food product. In the cities, one can't go 10 feet without seeing

Rabail Qadeer Baig, "A Burger Today, a Bypass Tomorrow," *Dawn*, December 9, 2006. Reproduced by permission.

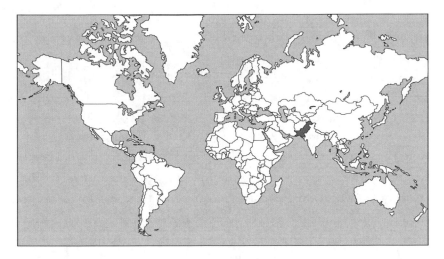

or smelling a restaurant or without coming face to face with a 20-foot-high billboard advertising junk food.

And yet, according to the National Nutrition Survey conducted by the UN [United Nations] in Pakistan during 2001–2002, to ascertain the recent level of the nutritional status, nearly half of the Pakistani population is suffering from micronutrient deficiencies, which ultimately lead to impaired immunity, diminished strength, vitality and lower mental and physical activity.

People usually gain weight during their college years. The bad news is that how college students eat dictates how they will eat after they graduate and how healthy they will be for the next 20 to 30 years.

Obesity in Pakistan

The National Nutrition Survey states that the most prevalent type of eating disorders, spreading rapidly in the young urban population of Pakistan, is overnutrition. Overnutrition is an excess of calories or excess/imbalance of nutrients. Overweight and obesity are the two major indicators of overnutrition. About one out of seven young adults in Pakistan are obese or overweight. Similarly, according to the National Health Survey 2001, the prevalence of obesity among adults aged 25–64 years, moving from low to middle to high socioeconomic status in urban areas is 21 per cent, 27 per cent and 42 per cent respectively.

The most affected are young students because their life is busy and they don't always have the time to fix a decent meal for themselves, and even if it is put together for them, they don't fancy eating it. Lack of time is the biggest excuse students have for not eating healthy food. "It is a real issue, and it's not going to go away," says Staci Nix, a foods and nutrition professor. "The college years are a prime time for students to develop lifelong habits. We need to teach these young men and women how to establish proper nutrition now, so they can live longer, happier and healthier lives."

The National Nutrition Survey states that the most prevalent type of eating disorders, spreading rapidly in the young urban population of Pakistan, is overnutrition.

Huma Quraishi, a young medical student in Karachi says she often grabs a pack of crisps or a cup of instant cappuccino for breakfast after staying up late the night before. But it's not what the students eat at home; it's what they choose to eat on campus.

"It seems like all the choices are greasy and full of fat," says Azeem Ahmad, another student, "but who wants to eat salad for lunch?" According to him, Pakistani men don't have to struggle with weight, for diets and salads are a girl's thing. "The greasier the food, the yummier," he says.

The Freshman 15

The problem is not so much the type of food as it is bad eating habits. Many college students in their freshman year are likely to gain at least 15 pounds, on average, because of their bad eating habits like ordering in junk food for dinner every night and snacking in between.

Pakistan's Obesity Problem

The burden of obesity is difficult to assess simply because very little research has been conducted in Pakistan. This is because whatever little resources that have been available to researchers, have been directed towards malnutrition, as opposed to obesity which is a relatively new phenomenon.

"The Obesity Challenge Initiating a Comprehensive Response,"
Dawn, *April 12, 2008.*

The cafeteria food does not help either. Local school, college and university canteens and cafeterias offer snacks which are unhygienic, fattening, and high in saturated fats and carbohydrates. One of the major problems in students' diets, as far as beverage consumption goes, is soft drinks. College students are attracted to them because they are easily accessible, cheap, and tasty. They may be convenient, but they cannot be categorised as good diet. They are full of sodium, sugar, and caffeine and cause dehydration among students because they drink too much of them.

Also, not many college students worry about a diet that would help them study better. Recent studies have shown that what students eat affects how clearly they think and concentrate; it also influences their intelligence level, memory and reaction time.

The Dangers of Fast Food

Fast food is the worst form of food as far as developing good study habits are concerned, as it is high in cholesterol and carbohydrates and affects a student's concentration or makes them lethargic. In addition, it often does not have the vitamins and minerals needed to keep the brain functioning at its best. The biggest problem is that most students don't even know what a healthy diet is, and a large percentage of students who are aware of proper nutrition choose to ignore it.

Disordered eating behaviours are complex problems, stemming from a variety of cultural, social, familial, psychological, and biological influences. Contrary to what many people think, these disorders are not just about food and weight issues. Rather, food and weight issues are symptoms of much more complicated, underlying problems in teenagers and young students.

There are many factors that contribute to the development of eating disorders in students, for example, stress, societal and family pressures, personality traits, underlying mood swings, anxiety, late-night study routines, socializing, etc. The media plays a huge role in promoting the junk food culture which attracts young students. As Jay Leno very rightly says, "A very famous fast-food chain announced that it's considering a more humane way of slaughtering its animals. You know they fatten them up and then kill them . . . the same thing they do to their customers."

Unhealthy eating habits cause malnutrition, as they do not have the right proportion of nutrients, which in turn impairs resistance to diseases, causes micronutrient deficiencies and increases the incidence of chronic or noncommunicable diseases. According to the National Health Survey, one out of every three persons over 45 years in Pakistan is suffering from high blood pressure. Approximately 2.7 million people have diabetes. It tends to increase with age and is more prevalent in women. Over 7.3 million people in Pakistan have elevated cholesterol levels requiring medical advice and intervention.

Focusing on Nutrition

The situation is grim, but it's never too late. But not balancing the good with the bad is contrary to what experts say is healthy. Good nutrition comes from consuming a wide array of foods. Vegetables and fruits are essential for vitamins and minerals. Experts say it is not necessary to cut out all greasy food, but it is advisable to consider eating an apple too, while grabbing a slice of pizza.

"If students are interested in getting the best out of their education, they'd better watch what they eat, and eat smart foods like soy, vegetables, fruits and seafood," says Sadia Rehman, a young nutritionist at a renowned hospital in Karachi.

In the end, remember, we are much more than what we eat, but what we eat can nevertheless help us to be much more than what we are.

Iron and vitamin B improve memory and study habits and so do iron-rich foods such as extra lean, red meat, cooked dried beans and dark green vegetables. Orange juice, rich in vitamin C, is also good to drink with iron-rich food to boost iron absorption. Drinking too much coffee and tea can reduce the level of iron in the body. Consumption of foods rich in vitamin B such as nonfat milk, bananas and seafood increases concentration and improves memory level and mental clarity.

Bad eating habits need to be changed and students should focus on eating smart food such as vegetables and food rich in fibre, iron and vitamin B. "Students should avoid taking 'low intelligence' snacks in great quantities or as daily meals," advises Rehman.

So next time you reach for a snack, ask yourself if you are eating something that will help you study. Smart eating is what makes you healthy in the long run and keeps you fit at the same time. To overcome eating disorders, "How to avoid bad eating habits" is a course all college students should take. It is essential to know what entails a good diet. If college students are unaware of what exactly a good diet is, bad eating habits are unavoidable. In the end, remember, we are much more than what we eat, but what we eat can nevertheless help us to be much more than what we are.

Inuit Obesity Problems Can Be Attributed to Global Warming

Catriona Davies

Catriona Davies is a staff writer for CNN.com. In the following viewpoint, she reports that climate change has significantly altered the hunting patterns and eating habits of the Inuit people who depend on the ice for their traditional diet of raw meat. Davies maintains that the melting ice and changing migratory patterns of animals have meant that Inuits are eating more junk food, resulting in more obesity and weight-related disease.

As you read, consider the following questions:

1. According to several studies, when will the Arctic Ocean become seasonally ice free?
2. How many people are estimated to live in the world's Arctic regions, as cited by the author?
3. According to the US National Snow and Ice Data Center, how far below the November 1979–2000 average of Arctic sea ice cover was November 2010's ice coverage?

Climate change is altering diets and lifestyles among Inuit people, according to a scientist who has studied the human face of global warming in the Arctic.

Barry Smit, a professor at the University of Guelph, Canada, has spent five years leading research projects into

Catriona Davies, "Inuit Lives and Diets Change as Ice Shifts," CNN.com, December 30, 2010. Reproduced by permission.

how melting ice and changes in wildlife habits are impacting the lives and livelihoods of far northern communities.

The Rising Popularity of Junk Food

Among his most striking findings was that increasing difficulty in hunting for traditional food was leading to much more junk food in the Inuit diet.

"People looking at the health of the Inuit have demonstrated that the traditional diet, which is almost exclusively raw meat, is in fact very healthy for them," Smit said. "But because of the new difficulties hunting, people are adapting their diets to what's available in the stores.

"The stores only have food that's easy to transport and doesn't perish, so there are no vegetables. The young people are increasingly eating highly processed junk food, so we are seeing more teeth problems and obesity."

Shifting Ice

The difficulties in hunting are caused by shifting ice and changing migratory patterns among animals such as seals, walrus, types of whales and polar bears, which form a large part of the traditional diet, Smit said.

He also noted that the shifting ice made hunting and traveling more dangerous.

Smit said: "Ice is fundamental to their livelihoods and culture. Most of their activities involve traveling on the ice.

The difficulties in hunting are caused by shifting ice and changing migratory patterns among animals such as seals, walrus, types of whales and polar bears, which form a large part of the traditional diet.

"Over the past decade or so, they have noticed that the behavior of the ice is changing, so their traditional roads are not as safe as they used to be."

He added: "They could be hunting on the edge of the ice and whole blocks of ice break off and drift out to sea, so they have immediate safety concerns."

This unpredictability undermines traditional knowledge of safe routes across the ice.

Social Implications

"There are social implications because the respect for elders has been maintained by their wisdom about when and where to travel on the ice," said Smit.

"But now elders will say it's safe to travel to a particular place at a certain time, and people have problems there. That undermines the traditional knowledge of the elders."

He added that houses built on permafrost were tipping as the ice shifted.

Tristan Pearce, one of Smit's researchers, also from the University of Guelph, who spent time with communities in Northwest Territories, Canada, said: "Due to thin, unstable, temporary sea ice cover that is vulnerable to winds and currents, aolagots (open boats) are becoming more common in winter months presenting new hunting opportunities and dangers to hunters."

He added: "Several studies project that the Arctic Ocean may become seasonally ice-free by the year 2040 or even earlier."

The ArcticNet Project

Smit studied Inuit as part of a Canadian project called Arctic-Net, and collaborated with scientists from other Arctic regions as part of the International Polar Year.

He led a team of researchers who built up-close relationships with communities in the Arctic, and invited people from those communities to join the project as co-researchers.

The Disappearance of the Traditional Diet

No one, not even residents of the northernmost villages on Earth, eats an entirely traditional northern diet anymore. Even the groups we came to know as Eskimo—which include the Inupiat and the Yupiks of Alaska, the Canadian Inuit and Inuvialuit, Inuit Greenlanders, and the Siberian Yupiks—have probably seen more changes in their diet in a lifetime than their ancestors did over thousands of years. The closer people live to towns and the more access they have to stores and cash-paying jobs, the more likely they are to have Westernized their eating. And with Westernization, at least on the North American continent, comes processed foods and cheap carbohydrates—Crisco, Tang, soda, cookies, chips, pizza, fries. "The young and urbanized," says Harriet Kuhnlein, director of the Centre for Indigenous Peoples' Nutrition and Environment at McGill University in Montreal, "are increasingly into fast food." So much so that type 2 diabetes, obesity, and other diseases of Western civilization are becoming causes for concern there too.

Patricia Gadsby,
"The Inuit Paradox,"
Discover, *October 2004.*

Smit said: "We have to document from the perspective of people who live in the Arctic how conditions are changing and how they are dealing with it to get a sense of how they might adapt in the future."

Four million people are estimated to live in the world's Arctic regions, across Canada, Alaska, Greenland, Norway and Russia, Smit said. In the far northern Arctic regions of Canada, the population is 85% Inuit, he added.

Climate Change

Smit said the average temperature rise since preindustrial time was conventionally estimated at 1.2 degrees Celsius globally, and 2–3 degrees Celsius in the Arctic.

The United States' National Snow and Ice Data Center reported that the extent of Arctic sea ice cover at the end of November this year [2010] was the second lowest on record, and 12% below the 1979–2000 average for November.

"You can look at a big map of the world and see the changes from climate change, but we are trying to put a local human face on this and find how people are affected and how they deal with it," said Smit.

A team of scientists, lead by Professor James J. Corbett of the University of Delaware published a paper in October [2010] warning that increased shipping as new ice-free sea routes opened up would further add to climate change in the Arctic.

Smit said opinions among the communities were divided on the implications of the opening up of shipping routes through the Arctic Ocean, speeding up oil, gas and mineral exploration and tourism.

"If you look over the next couple of decades, the transformation will be huge. It won't be an Arctic environment at all and people will have to modify their way of life completely," he said.

Italy's Obesity Trend Is Exacerbated by Rising Food Prices

Marcus Walker

Marcus Walker is a reporter for the Wall Street Journal. *In the following viewpoint, he contends that the rising prices of such Italian food staples as bread, pasta, and vegetables have precipitated a shift toward more affordable processed foods high in fat, sugar, and salt for many Italians. Walker reports that obesity is increasing in all demographics of Italian society, especially among children.*

As you read, consider the following questions:

1. According to Walker, how much did the price of pasta jump in Italy in 2008?
2. What percentage of Italian adults were obese in 2005, as cited by Walker?
3. According to Walker, what percentage of Italian preadolescents are overweight or obese?

Rome—The United Nations hosts a global summit in Rome today to discuss a food-price crisis that has triggered riots in poor countries and toppled Haiti's government. But the land of saltimbocca alla romana has food troubles of its own.

Marcus Walker, "Arrivederci, Penne? Food Inflation Takes Its Toll on the Italian Diet," *Wall Street Journal*, June 3, 2008. Reprinted with permission of *The Wall Street Journal*.

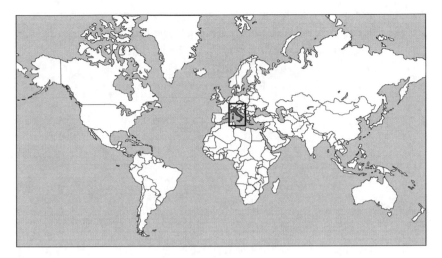

And they are hitting Ernesta Santirocco in the form of soaring pasta prices, which her $678 pension can't cover, she complains. Leaving one of the German Lidl discount grocery stores packed with cheaper, processed foods, she notes—not very proudly—that her shopping bags contain "schifezze," Italian for disgusting things.

They are also unhealthy. The soaring costs of pasta, bread, fruit and vegetables are making Italy's famed Mediterranean diet harder to afford in a country that prides itself on its healthy cuisine. Italians, in turn, are dining more on cheap processed foods high in fat, sugar and salt. The consumption of those foods may be accelerating a trend toward higher levels of diabetes and heart disease, while starkly clarifying the supersized cost of good health.

The soaring costs of pasta, bread, fruit and vegetables are making Italy's famed Mediterranean diet harder to afford in a country that prides itself on its healthy cuisine.

Some, noting that obesity rates among low-income families have soared in the U.S. and Europe, fret that fewer people can afford the fruits and vegetables that lead to better health.

**Percentage Increase in Price and Decrease
In Consumption of Foods in Italy, 2006–2007**

	Price %	Consumption %
Vegetables	6.8	–4.2
Fruits	8.3	–2.5
Bread	13.1	–6.2
Pasta	18.6	–2.6

TAKEN FROM: Marcus Walker, "Arrivederci, Penne?
Food Inflation Takes Its Toll on the Italian Diet,"
Wall Street Journal, June 3, 2008.

Such fresh foods are more susceptible to rises in commodity prices, such as energy, which make up a smaller percentage of costs in processed foods.

"The global trend is rising prices of fresh fruit and vegetable versus processed foods," says France Caillavet, nutritionist at the National Institute for Agricultural Research in Paris. In France, too, she says, "many poor households now can't afford a healthy diet."

In Italy, food prices are up 5.7% in the past year, including a 7% rise in fruit prices and a 20% jump in the price of pasta—almost as steep as the 26% rise in gasoline prices. Since 2006, six out of 10 households in Italy have adjusted what they eat in response to the rising cost of fresh produce, according to a study by the Italian agricultural confederation.

People aren't starving or rioting in Italy. But the high prices are likely to accelerate a troubling health trend, nutritionists say. Over 12% of Italian adults were obese in 2005, according to the World Health Organization's latest available figures. That's far below obesity rates of well over 30% in the U.S., but it's up from around 7% in Italy a decade earlier. The WHO's latest estimate predates the recent food-price jump.

As pasta al pomodoro loses ground to French fries, Italy's relatively low level of obesity is surging among children. Around one-third of preadolescents are now overweight or obese, making them among the plumpest in Europe, according to researchers at the International Obesity TaskForce.

"Ten years ago, obesity was rare; now it's accelerating in all groups," says Pietro Antonio Migliaccio, Italy's best-known diet doctor, who frequently appears on daytime TV urging Italians to adhere to their traditional recipes. A decade ago at Prof. Migliaccio's clinic, his heaviest-duty scales for weighing his clients only went up to 220 pounds. Now, his scales go up to 550 pounds.

Sedentary lifestyles, working mothers, splintering families and the pull of American fast-food culture have all contributed to growing girths along the shores of southern Europe in recent years. Now rising food prices are making more people change their diets and will compound Italy's growing obesity problem if prices stay high, says Prof. Migliaccio. "The Mediterranean diet is still the best thing against weight gain, cardiovascular disease and aging," he says. That message is getting drowned out by rising prices, as well as by cultural changes. At the Pewex supermarket in a working-class suburb of Rome, Emanuela Lo Giudice fills her shopping cart with convenience food and 1.5 liter bottles of Coca-Cola. "I'm taking whatever is on special offer," the mother of four says. Fresh fruit and vegetables no longer feature much in the dinners she prepares—too costly on her salary of a little under $1,900 a month. "It's absurd that they cost so much," she says.

Rome's colorful fruit and vegetable stalls, and other specialized stores selling fresh products such as bread and fish, are losing business. "People aren't shopping for quality anymore," says Carlo Pompei, who runs a fruit and vegetable store in an inner-city neighborhood.

Stores like Lidl have relatively little fresh food, but give plenty of space to soft drinks, chips, and other processed foods rich in calories but low in nutritional value.

The Catholic Church is jumping to the rescue of struggling Romans and of the Mediterranean diet. In May, the Church's relief organization, Caritas, opened a pilot charity supermarket. Customers get a means-tested number of tokens per month with which they can pay for food and beverages. Caritas normally serves Rome's homeless, mentally ill or alcoholic down-and-outs. The Church hasn't had to feed low-income families in its hometown since the Great Depression.

Periodical and Internet Sources Bibliography

The following articles have been selected to supplement the diverse views presented in this chapter.

Shahreen Abedin — "The Social Side of Obesity: You Are Who You Eat With," *Time*, September 3, 2009.

BBC News — "Sleep Patterns Affect Weight Loss," March 29, 2011. www.bbc.co.uk.

Hugh Collins — "Obesity and Ethnicity—Hispanic Women Suffering More than Once Thought," *Hugh Collins* (blog), April 22, 2010. http://hughcollins.word press.com.

Erik German and Solana Pyne — "Brazilians Pack on the Pounds," GlobalPost, November 25, 2010. www.globalpost.com.

Wil Haygood — "Kentucky Town of Manchester Illustrates National Obesity Crisis," *Washington Post*, July 12, 2010.

Ashley Luthern — "The Culture of Obesity," *Food & Think* (blog), July 8, 2009. http://blogs.smithsonianmag.com.

Mark MacKinnon — "'Curse of Affluence' Causing Obesity Crisis in Wealthy Middle East," *Toronto Globe & Mail*, September 26, 2008.

Michael Mosley — "The Brains Behind the Obesity Problem," BBC News, January 25, 2011. www.bbc.co.uk.

Newsweek — "The Real Cause of Obesity," September 10, 2009.

Michael Slackman — "Privilege Pulls Qatar Toward Unhealthy Choices," *New York Times*, April 26, 2010.

US News & World Report — "Obesity Tied to Education, Income, but Not Suburbia: Study," February 10, 2011.

CHAPTER 3

Obesity Effects

The Global Obesity Problem Decreases Life Expectancy for Kids

Medical News

Medical News is a website that collects the latest medical news stories. In the following viewpoint, the toll obesity takes on children is explored. Studies have shown that obesity shortens life expectancy in children because they have a much greater chance of developing weight-related diseases such as diabetes and heart disease. Furthermore, obesity lessens the quality of life as well as threatens an individual's psychological health and well-being.

As you read, consider the following questions:

1. By how many years do experts predict obesity may shorten a child's life expectancy?
2. According to the viewpoint, what percentage of obese children between the ages of ten and fifteen continue to be obese at twenty-five?
3. How is an obese child's quality of life damaged by obesity, as stated in the viewpoint?

For the first time in history, the next generation will not live longer, or even as long, as their parents.

"Diseases such as type II diabetes, high blood pressure, heart conditions and joint deterioration—what were once considered 'adult' diseases—are regularly being diagnosed in children, due to the prevalence of obesity," said Jessica Bartfield, MD, internal medicine and medical weight-loss specialist at Gottlieb Memorial Hospital, part of the Loyola University Health System.

The earlier obesity develops in children, the more severe it tends to be as an adult.

Effects of Obesity

"What is particularly tragic is that studies have suggested that obesity in children today may contribute to a 2–5 year decline in their life expectancy, shorter than that of their parents, due to obesity-related diseases that are largely preventable," said Dr. Bartfield, who is part of Gottlieb's medically supervised weight-loss program involving physicians, nutritionists, exercise physiologists and behavioralists.

She says the causes are "multifactorial, including environment and culture." Genetics and parental weight status also play a role.

"If one parent is obese, a child has a 50 percent likelihood of being obese, and if both parents are obese, that skyrockets to 80 percent likelihood," she said.

Research by the Centers for Disease Control [and Prevention] found that 80 percent of obese children between the ages of 10–15 continue to be obese at age 25. Furthermore, the earlier obesity develops in children, the more severe it tends to be as an adult.

In addition to health implications, there are psychological and social damages as well.

"In addition to decreasing years of life, obesity decreases the quality of life through social ostracism, bullying, social isolation, and poor self-esteem which can lead to poor performance in school, in jobs and in life," she said.

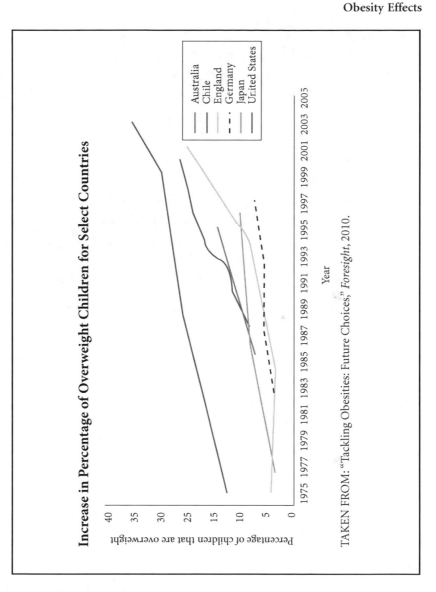

Increase in Percentage of Overweight Children for Select Countries

Legend:
Australia
Chile
England
Germany
Japan
United States

Percentage of children that are overweight: 40 35 30 25 15 10 5 0

Year: 1975 1977 1979 1981 1983 1985 1987 1989 1991 1993 1995 1997 1999 2001 2003 2005

TAKEN FROM: "Tackling Obesities: Future Choices," *Foresight*, 2010.

Top Five Ways to Reverse the Obesity Trend

1. Parents take charge. "Focus on getting the family healthy, not putting someone on a diet," she said. "Monitor and take accountability for what the family is eating. Plan meals, set limits and take the team approach."

2. Involve the kids. "As a family, create a weekly meal plan, look up calorie counts, make a grocery list, read product labels, choose fresh rather than packaged and get everyone's participation," said Dr. Bartfield. "Everyone has to get on board to be successful."

3. Add fresh fruits and vegetables. "Replace applesauce for oil in baked goods, add carrots, broccoli and kale to soups and omelettes, cut up fresh fruit as a side dish," said Dr. Bartfield. "Even if it is dipped in low-calorie whipped topping or low-calorie salad dressing (moderately) to make the fruit or vegetable more ap- pealing to kids."

4. Cut liquid calories. "Soda, flavored and full fat milk, fruit punches and fruit-flavored beverages are loaded in sugar and empty calories," says Dr. Bartfield. "Substitute 2 percent for whole milk, or skim for 2 percent, and try adding water, seltzer or club soda to juices to cut calo- ries."

5. Prioritize breakfast and keep meals consistent. "Eating within the first hour of waking up powers the brain and jump-starts the metabolism for the rest of the day," said Dr. Bartfield. "Choose protein and fiber in breakfast foods to boost endurance." Establish set meal times, and calories per meal, and stick to them, with defined healthy options for snacking.

Keeping It Real

"In overweight children with medical complications or obese children, strive for a one-pound individual weight loss per month," said Dr. Bartfield, who uses guidelines by the Ameri- can Academy of Pediatrics. "Focus on weight maintenance for overweight kids without medical complications. As kids con- tinue to grow in height, their percentage Body Mass Index (BMI) on the growth chart will decrease."

The Global Obesity Crisis Will Contribute to Escalating Food Prices

Hollie Shaw

Hollie Shaw is a reporter for the Financial Post. *In the following viewpoint, she discusses the findings of a recent report that finds that as a result of a burgeoning middle class and a rise in obesity around the world, food prices will inevitably rise. Experts predict that as more middle-class consumers enter the market there will be a change in food-consumption patterns, as rising obesity in emerging markets will spark a trend for healthier, high-value foods that will put a strain on resources and spike food prices.*

As you read, consider the following questions:

1. As stated by Shaw, how many new consumers are added to the middle class each year?

2. How much of an increase in corn prices were biofuels responsible for between 2002 and 2008, as described by Shaw?

3. According to Shaw, what percentage of the global trade in soybeans will China buy in 2001–2012?

Hollie Shaw, "Middle Class Drives Food Prices," *Financial Post*, January 12, 2011. Material reprinted with the express permission of National Post Inc.

Food will become much more expensive in the next decade thanks to a burgeoning middle class around the world, says a new consumer report from Deloitte Touche Tohmatsu.

"Greater consumption leads to a greater strain on resources," says the Consumer 2020 report [referring to "Consumer 2020: Reading the Signs"], presented this week [in January 2011] at the National Retail Federation in New York. "Without sustainable consumption, it will become increasingly difficult to meet the collective expectations and aspirations of the world's new consumers."

Food-Consumption Patterns

The report, which projects shifts in consumer behaviour related to demographic, economic and technological influences, says the growing affluence of the middle classes in emerging markets is set to dramatically change food-consumption patterns.

In the next decade, the world's population is projected to rise 11%, but the growth in the middle classes is what will affect food supply and prices, the report says: At least 70 million new consumers around the world will be added to the middle class each year, reaching 800 million by 2020.

That is largely due to the boom in emerging markets such as China. "As incomes rise, people typically shift from grain-based diets to diets dominated by 'high-value' foods such as fruit, vegetables, meat, dairy products and fish," the report says. Booming economies can lead to ballooning waistlines, with technology and development in emerging markets spurring a dietary shift to more processed foods.

China's economy has grown 9% to 10% a year despite the recession, and Chinese have flocked to urban areas and more white-collar jobs. "This has allowed for more spending on food, including Western-style fatty and sugary fast foods, drinks, prepared meals and packaged goods," the report says.

The Demand for Healthier Foods

Rising obesity in emerging markets will likely spark a trend mirroring greater demand for healthy and "functional" foods with nutritional benefit. Those "varied high-value foods" will put a greater strain on resources, the survey predicts.

Booming economies can lead to ballooning waistlines, with technology and development in emerging markets spurring a dietary shift to more processed foods.

"The significant pressure on crop yields and meat production globally will continue to keep food prices high. Food prices will rise further due to the limited availability of suitable land and water, as well as the reduction of global grain stocks due to a number of climate-influenced poor harvests in different parts of the world and new demands for biofuel production."

Biofuels were primarily responsible for the 105% increase in corn prices between 2002 and 2008, the report noted. As food prices rise, many consumers will be more selective about what they buy and will not be able to spend as much money at restaurants. The report also cautions that climbing food prices might require government intervention in many parts of the world.

As consumers in various parts of the world face "the potential reality of empty retail shelves," it could lead to political instability, price inflation and even food riots of the kind seen in places such as Haiti, Morocco and Pakistan in 2008.

Last week [January 2–8], the United Nations' food agency (FAO [Food and Agriculture Organization]) reported that food prices hit a record high in December [2010], higher than the riot-plagued period of 2008.

The report comes after a year of price spikes in agricultural commodities largely due to poor weather, which tightened supply and drove up prices. Last year, U.S. wheat futures prices jumped 47%, corn climbed above 50% and soybeans rose 34%.

In addition to bad weather, increased Asian demand is fuelling the spike; it is predicted China will buy 60% of the global trade in soybeans in 2011–2012 twice what it purchased of the commodity just four years ago.

"Such instances make it painfully clear that the additional demands of the new middle class for food will require much better management of land, water, supplies, waste and farming practices," the Deloitte report notes.

The Global Obesity Problem Is Being Sensationalized for Political Gain

Martin O'Neill

Martin O'Neill is an author and political philosopher. In the following viewpoint, he contends that British government pronouncements about obesity—especially one putting it on the same level as climate change—have been hyperbolic and apocalyptic. O'Neill questions the way government officials are sensationalizing the problem of obesity, contending that it does a disservice to the urgency and importance of addressing climate change, which he views as a much more critical issue.

As you read, consider the following questions:

1. As stated by the author, what did the British health minister claim about the problem of obesity?

2. What does the Foresight report on obesity claim about the prevalence of obesity in the United Kingdom by 2050?

3. What does the author say the claim that obesity will lead to children dying before their parents really mean?

Shakespeare's Julius Caesar was able to see the upside of obesity in a way that would be unimaginable for our contemporary politicians.

Current rhetoric about the weight of the nation has, indeed, tended towards the hyperbolic and apocalyptic.

There is much talk of an "obesity time bomb", and of an "epidemic of obesity" that challenges both the longevity not to mention the public finances of the nation [Great Britain].

An Absurd Comparison

In stark contrast to Caesar's sanguine feelings about expanding waistlines, last week [October 14–20, 2007] saw perhaps the most delightfully absurd pronouncement on this epidemic of fatness when Health Minister Alan Johnson claimed that obesity was a "potential crisis on the scale of climate change".

It is worth stopping for a second to appreciate the sheer silliness of Alan Johnson's claim. It is certainly true that the spread of obesity may curtail the upwards progress of life expectancy in the developed world, and may diminish the quality of life of many of the world's affluent citizens through contributing to life years spent coping with diabetes or coronary heart disease. But even this unhappy prospect pales into insignificance when compared with the dangers of climate change.

Obesity is a problem of the affluent, comfortable, and (overly) well-fed, whereas those who will bear the brunt of climate change are the world's poorest and most disadvantaged.

Flooding and extreme weather have the capacity to cause hundreds of thousands of deaths throughout the world, whilst desertification and rising sea levels have the capacity to displace tens of millions of people from their homes, leading to war, famine and unpredictable political upheavals.

Obesity is a problem of the affluent, comfortable, and (overly) well-fed, whereas those who will bear the brunt of climate change are the world's poorest and most disadvantaged.

Stop the Obesity Hyperbole

If obesity is among the worst problems faced by a nation, then what this tells us is that this nation is actually doing rather well. Johnson's remarks equate the lifestyle problems of the world's wealthy with the real matters of imminent life and death that are faced by the world's poor.

It does a disservice to the importance of action on climate change to bracket it alongside problems caused by eating too much and not getting enough exercise.

It is not so much that the government's response to obesity is itself nonsensical, but that much of the way it is reported and communicated is hysterical or confused.

The report of Foresight, the government's science think tank, on "Tackling Obesities: Future Choices" contains a good deal of sober analysis about the social, environmental and physiological mechanisms that lead to obesity, together with different proposals for how the problem might be tackled.

It is not so much that the government's response to obesity is itself nonsensical, but that much of the way it is reported and communicated is hysterical or confused.

The Blame Game

But discussion of the causal processes that increase the likelihood of obesity seem always to be stuck in an overly simplistic dichotomy—either it's a matter of individual choice, and hence nothing to do with government, or else it's the inevitable consequence of modern life, and therefore something for which individuals are not responsible.

The Foresight report attempted to make a number of nuanced points, but the predictable reaction from the media was that this meant that obesity "is not the fault of individuals" or, as John Humphrys put it, somewhat mysteriously, on the *Today* programme, people are obese because "our biology is out of step with the abundance and convenience offered by the modern environment". (As if we might have expected "our biology" to have kept up with the modern world, and are free of the responsibility to make better choices in any circumstance in which it has failed to do so!)

Reasonable debate about social problems related to problems of addiction and unwise choices seem stuck in a rather reductive "blame game". But the plausible positions in this area are neither the unsophisticated determinist view that sees obesity as nothing at all to do with fault or choice, nor the avowedly tough-minded (but hopelessly simplistic) position that sees this as a realm of individual choice untouched by broader issues of social policy.

The Role of Personal Choices

In fact, there is nothing inconsistent in thinking that certain problems can result from individual's choices (whether those problems are obesity, addiction, alcohol abuse or whatever else) whilst at the same time allowing that certain sorts of environmental and social backgrounds make some choices easier than others.

The overly reductive question of that asks who is "at fault" or "to blame" for problems like these needs to be pulled apart. There are causal questions here that range over issues about social, environmental and psychological mechanisms.

There are also irreducibly normative questions about who should bear the costs of these problems, and what should be done by governments and by individuals to tackle them. Good answers here will be boringly complex (like the Foresight re-

"Obesity problem is becoming a global problem," cartoon by Wilfred Hildonen, www.CartoonStock.com. Copyright © Wilfred Hildonen. Reproduction rights obtainable from www.CartoonStock.com.

port itself). Easier answers tend to suggest lazy thinking, but easy answers make better headlines.

The Foresight Report

This is not to say that there is nothing with which one might quibble in the government's "Tackling Obesities" report.

Firstly, there is the bizarre pluralisation: from "obesity" to "obesities": a piece of willful jargon-making without justification.

Secondly, one needs to be very careful when reading research that makes claims such as "if current trends continue, most people in the UK [United Kingdom] will be obese by 2050".

Social trends, like economic trends, are malleable, unpredictable and subject to reversal. For example, current trends in obesity are not themselves 45 years old, which might suggest the debatable wisdom of projecting them 45 years into the future without severe caveats.

Conditional claims that turn around substantial hypotheticals such as this need to be read as what they are, not as confident scientific predictions for how things will certainly be. A bit of reticence in making some of these big claims could hopefully only add to the plausibility of the overall analysis.

An Alarmist Claim

There is one claim, though, that should be excluded from further debate without further delay, in part because it seems to be irredeemably subject to misinterpretation. Again and again we hear that the spread of obesity will lead to "children dying before their parents".

This conjures up visions of a generation of obese children who will predecease their mothers and fathers.

But what is actually meant is simply that, with the growth of obesity, life expectancy might drop in such a way that many people will die at a younger age than their parents did. Whilst this is still, of course, an unpleasant prospect, it isn't quite the horrific vista of losing a generation to obesity.

If claims like this aren't made carefully, they can sound shrill and alarmist—fine, perhaps, for grabbing headlines, but not so good for reasoned reflection on difficult matters of policy.

Alan Johnson's remarks about obesity and climate change bring to mind an altogether more sensible pronouncement on fatness from George Bernard Shaw. As Shaw rightly pointed out, "no diet will remove all the fat from your body because the brain is entirely fat. Without a brain, you might look good, but all you could do is run for public office." Alan Johnson might give a bit more thought to his public utterances if he isn't to end up unwittingly proving Shaw to be all too correct.

Many in India Are Turning to Bariatric Surgery to Combat Obesity

Sanchita Sharma

Sanchita Sharma is a reporter for the Hindustan Times. *In the following viewpoint, she observes that the practice of bariatric surgery to treat obesity has spiked in popularity in India, a country with a growing obesity crisis. Sharma notes that many overweight and obese Indians choose to try to lose weight without surgery, turning to exercise and nutritional counseling to control their weight.*

As you read, consider the following questions:

1. According to the viewpoint, how many cases of bariatric surgery were there in India from January–November 2010?

2. How many people in the world are obese, as stated in the viewpoint?

3. As noted in the viewpoint, what percentage of diabetes cases worldwide are linked to overweight and obesity?

If bariatric surgery to treat obesity is a barometer, obesity is a rapidly ballooning problem in India. People taking recourse to this surgery to lose weight has risen over 2000 per-

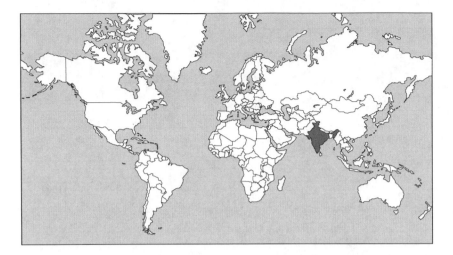

cent in the last four years. From just 150 cases in 2006 to 3,500 cases by the end of November 2010. Bariartric surgery—which costs between Rs 1.5 to Rs 2 lakh—involves reducing the size of the stomach using reversible gastric banding to make people feel full after a small meal, bringing down their appetite by two-thirds.

"Too much food and inactivity are feeding the genetic predisposition to weight gain, making one in three urban adults obese," says Dr Pradeep Chowbey, director of the Max Institute of Minimal Access, Metabolic and Bariatric Surgery, where 25–30 surgeries are done every month.

Problem of Plenty

The problem of rising obesity is not unique to India. At least 2.6 million people die each year as a result of being overweight or obese. That makes obesity a bigger killer than malnutrition, shows World Health Organization data. Body mass index (BMI)—the weight in kilograms divided by the square of the height in meters (kg/m2)—is used to classify overweight and obesity in adults.

For Indians and south Asians, being overweight means having a BMI equal to or more than 23, and obesity is equal to or more than 27. Globally, one billion adults are overweight and more than 300 million are obese. If they don't change their lifestyle, this number will surpass 1.5 billion by 2015.

On Friday, Dr Chowbey has discharged a 26-year-old man who weighed 230 kg, "He was so overweight that he could not sit in a chair or climb stairs. After the laparoscopic surgery, he's looking forward to losing 6–8 kg a month till he reaches his desired weight," said Chowbey, who recommends surgery for only those with a BMI of over 32.5.

The problem of rising obesity is not unique to India. At least 2.6 million people die each year as a result of being overweight or obese.

Lose and Win

Most people do not need to take the surgery route. Nutritionist Naini Setalvad, 47, counsels people on how to lose weight and keep it off, from her Napean Sea Road clinic in south Mumbai. The 60 kg 5'2″ Setalvad speaks from experience, having lost and kept off 100 kg for 15 years.

"I have been battling obesity since I was 13, when addiction to sweets and fried food pushed up my weight to 90 kg. Despite my swimming, gymming and trying every possible diet plan, it kept rising, touching an incredible 160 kg when I was 23," said Setalvad.

Unable to function normally—"I did not travel for a decade because I could not take flights or get into a bus or on train"—Setalvad decided to learn more about nutrition at the age of 32. She is now 47 and weighs 60kg.

"Aerobic exercises for two hours a day and my newfound nutritional knowledge helped me lose weight and keep it off. I also had to undergo body sculpting to lose excess skin after weight loss. Surgery is usually needed if you lose more than 50 kg," she said.

What Is Bariatric Surgery?

Weight loss surgery is a serious surgical procedure that decreases the size of the stomach, reduces food intake and can enable you to lose a significant amount of weight. It is a permanent procedure that requires a lifetime commitment to maintaining a healthy lifestyle.

Consumer Guide to Bariatric Surgery, *2010.*

While Setalvad did it alone, Rashmi Abhyankar, 31, took the help of VLCC to shed over 20 kg in less than three months. "When I joined VLCC, I was 27 and weighed 82 kg. I was down to 61 kg in three months, but it was regular follow-ups with the counselor that helped me stay off oily snacks, which were the cause of my weight gain," said Abhyankar, who now weighs 59 kg.

"Some people can do it alone, but I initially needed the constant counselling and guidance. I once broke down and cried when my weight plateaued and came close to giving up, but now I manage on my own," says Setalvad.

"People now want to adopt a healthy lifestyle to feel and not just look good. That has led to VLCC growing from one centre in 1989 to over 225 centres across 90 cities in India. And 16 centres in 7 other countries," said Dr Veena Aggarwal, Head R&D, VLCC Group.

Healthy Ever After

Limiting total fat intake and shifting fat consumption away from saturated fats (oils that solidify at room temperature and those found in processed foods) to unsaturated fats, eating more fruit, vegetables, pulses, whole grains and nuts, and limit the intake of sugar and salt for a start. That, along with one hour of moderate-intensity physical activity seven days a week reduces the risk of heart disease, diabetes, colon and breast cancers.

Globally, 44 percent of diabetes, 23 percent of heart disease and 7–41 percent of certain cancers are linked with overweight and obesity. "If options of diet, exercising for an hour a day, drugs and surgery are applied at lower levels of obesity, heart disease and diabetes can be prevented in nearly 15 percent of the adult population of India (nearly 7 crore people)," said Dr Anoop Misra, director, department of diabetes and metabolic diseases, Fortis hospitals.

The Irish Health System Will Be Burdened by Chronic Health Conditions Caused by Obesity

Lisa Smyth

Lisa Smyth is reporter for the Belfast Telegraph. *In the following viewpoint, she presents the findings of a 2010 Institute of Public Health (IPH) report that states that a range of chronic health conditions will become more prevalent in Northern Ireland in the coming years. Smyth reports that an expected increase in rates of diabetes, heart disease, hypertension, and strokes— conditions often linked to the rise of obesity—will have a dire economic effect on the country's health services.*

As you read, consider the following questions:

1. According to the Institute of Public Health in Ireland, how many people across the province will suffer from a chronic illness by 2020?
2. What recommendations did the Stormont health committee propose to tackle the growing problem of obesity in Northern Ireland?
3. According to Michael McBride, how many deaths every year does obesity cause in Northern Ireland?

Lisa Smyth, "Health Timebomb: Life-Threatening Conditions Could Collapse NHS," *Belfast Telegraph*, March 16, 2010. Reproduced by permission.

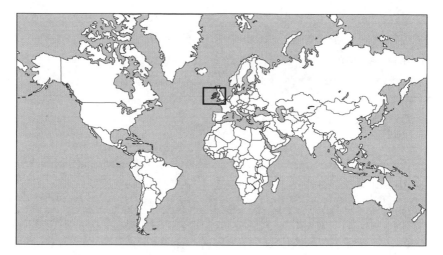

Life-threatening conditions such as diabetes, coronary heart disease, high blood pressure and strokes are set to rise in Northern Ireland by over 30% in the next decade.

A damning report into the future state of the health of people across the province has warned a range of chronic health conditions are to increase dramatically in coming years.

The IPH Report

According to the new study carried out by the Institute of Public Health (IPH) in Ireland, an additional 145,000 people across the province will suffer from a chronic illness by 2020, which experts have warned could push the already over-stretched health service to breaking point.

The figures have been released as the health service in Northern Ireland faces its biggest financial threat in years and it is believed initiatives to help patients manage chronic conditions could be axed as part of an additional £113m[illion] savings the Department of Health, Social Services and Public Safety must find.

The report has called into question the effectiveness of the Government's multimillion-pound public health strategy— aimed at educating and promoting good health—at a time when every penny counts.

Alarming Results

"This report shows some frightening statistics," chair of the British Medical Association's Northern Ireland Council Dr Paul Darragh said.

"The figures point to an alarming increase in the numbers of people living with hypertension, coronary heart disease, stroke and diabetes.

"We are facing a chronic disease epidemic over the next 10 years due, in part, to the increasing ageing population and levels of obesity in Northern Ireland.

"This poses a huge challenge to our health and social care system and economy.

"The predicted rise in chronic diseases will place greater demands on GPs [medical doctors] and primary care services, as well as our local hospitals as more unwell patients need to be treated.

"This is unsustainable given the increasing financial constraints that the health service is facing.

"Prevention programmes have already proved successful in reducing the death rate from heart disease in Northern Ireland.

"We need to give an increased role to primary prevention of these chronic debilitating and ultimately life-terminating conditions. Our children, our future, deserve no less."

Considering the Risk Factors

Poverty, unemployment, the environment, smoking, alcohol consumption, diet and physical activity are known risk factors for chronic disease and these are distributed unevenly across society.

The IPH study found that socioeconomic circumstances strongly affect the prevalence of chronic conditions in an area.

For all the chronic conditions considered in the study, people living in more deprived areas are more likely to be affected.

More Education and Help Are Vital

Andrew Dougal, chief executive of NI [Northern Ireland] Chest, Heart & Stroke [Association] (NICHSA), said while messages conveying the importance of a healthy lifestyle in preventing chronic conditions has been well received by the middle class, more must be done to educate and assist people living in poverty.

"We see a need for much more funding for long-term conditions," he said.

"NICHSA has developed a self-management programme for people with long-term conditions and we would hope that will be made available across Northern Ireland.

"Showing people how to manage their condition greatly reduces the number of unnecessary admissions and readmissions to hospitals.

"Investing in the voluntary sector provides value for money but unfortunately when budgets are cut the voluntary sector is usually the hardest hit but I believe that is a false economy."

The Challenges to Better Care

Health Minister Michael McGimpsey said he is committed to ensuring the best quality and value of health and social care services for Northern Ireland but is faced with the challenge of having to fight for the health service as demand is growing at a much faster rate than funding.

"What this report highlights is that, certainly in the short to medium term, chronic conditions will continue to rise and place increasing demands on our already stretched service," he said.

"In the last two years, there has been an increase of over 20% in demand for hospital services yet our funding has only increased by 0.5% in real terms.

"This is further compounded by the fact that my department is already working to deliver efficiency savings of some £700m.

"Recently, I have been tasked with delivering further savings of £113m. This is while trying to close a funding gap of almost £600m in health spending which Northern Ireland faces when compared to England."

Emphasis Needs to Be on Prevention

Placing more emphasis on prevention and tackling health inequalities would reduce cases of heart disease, stroke and type 2 diabetes by 80%, it has been claimed.

Chief executive of the Institute of Public Health in Ireland Dr Jane Wilde said cases of chronic illness could be significantly cut by the elimination of major risk factors such as obesity and stress.

Her comments come as a leading Northern Ireland GP called on people to make simple changes to their lifestyle which could ultimately save their lives.

Dr Theo Nugent, a member of the British Medical Association's Northern Ireland Council, recently addressed the Department of Culture, Arts and Leisure on how to encourage more people to exercise.

Chief executive of the Institute of Public Health in Ireland Dr Jane Wilde said cases of chronic illness could be significantly cut by the elimination of major risk factors such as obesity and stress.

"It is important to get the message across that making small changes can significantly reduce the risk of suffering from a chronic illness," he said.

Obesity in Northern Ireland

Obesity rates have increased by 50% in a decade. Specifically with regard to obesity:

- 250,000 people in Northern Ireland are clinically obese

- 9% of 16–19-year-olds are obese

- 12% of 20–29-year-olds are obese

- 14% of 30–39-year-olds are obese

- 22% of 40–49-year-olds are obese

- 25% of over 50-year-olds are obese

Tackling obesity could save the health service in Northern Ireland £8.4 million, reduce sickness absence by 170,000 days and add an extra ten years of life onto an individual's life span.

British Medical Association Northern Ireland,
"Background: Obesity in Northern Ireland,"
Position Paper on Obesity in Northern Ireland, *June 2010.*

"A major factor of improving health is exercise and I believe we need to be working to demystify exercise so it is no longer associated with elite athletes.

"It can be accessible to everyone.

"Doing something like leaving the car at home and walking to work can make a huge difference and is easy to achieve. You don't have to pay for expensive gym membership and you don't need lots of specialized equipment."

Prevention Is Key

And continuing on the theme of prevention, Dr Wilde said: "Chronic diseases cause early death, immense suffering and reduce quality of life.

"Prevention makes sense. Policy makers and Government need to place much stronger emphasis on prevention and tackling health inequalities."

"We already have Government policies and strategies to promote healthier lifestyles and strengthen the early assessment and diagnosis of chronic conditions.

"These are welcome but all the evidence suggests that we need much broader focus.

"We need to think about prevention right across the life course, to focus particularly on early childhood and the needs of vulnerable and disadvantaged people.

"Understanding current need and future prevalence and how it varies with factors such as age, sex, geography and local socioeconomic circumstances is essential for good planning and monitoring of chronic disease management.

"We need a full debate about how we achieve much greater success in prevention.

"Already we have shown the dramatic fall in the death rates for heart disease.

"This means thinking about what services we want, how prevention can be more effective and how we can ensure that at all ages we do what we know works well."

Report Latest in Long Line of Stark Warnings for People of Province

The report by the Institute of Public Health (IPH) is the latest stark warning of the health timebomb facing men, women and children in Northern Ireland.

Last November it emerged two-thirds of men and 50% of women across Northern Ireland are expected to be clinically obese by 2050.

The figures were contained in a report drawn up by the Stormont health committee which warned the health complications linked to obesity could lead to the collapse of the health service.

The Stormont health committee proposed a series of recommendations to tackle the growing problem of obesity in Northern Ireland—including compulsory physical education classes for all schoolchildren, restrictions on advertising foods with high levels of salt, sugar and fat, and the traffic light labelling system [a label that uses color coding to show the amount of fat, sugar, salt and saturates in a product] becoming the norm on all food sold across the province.

Last November [2009] it emerged two-thirds of men and 50% of women across Northern Ireland are expected to be clinically obese by 2050.

Speaking at the time, Jim Wells, chair of the committee, said: "One of the points that has been raised in the debate is the fact that this generation could have a shorter life span than the previous generation because of obesity and that would be the first time this has happened.

"We are quite literally eating ourselves to death. This is a ticking timebomb and action must be taken urgently to address this issue. The health service will collapse under the strain if action is not taken."

Just two months earlier, Northern Ireland's chief medical officer Michael McBride revealed the impact of obesity causes around 450 deaths every year and reduces life expectancy by up to nine years.

Obesity is a major contributing factor to a range of chronic diseases, such as hypertension and type 2 diabetes.

Both the Northern Ireland Chest, Heart & Stroke Association (NICHSA) and British Heart Foundation have called for a single, consistent food labelling scheme using the traffic light system to help consumers make healthier choices when buying food.

Asian Rates of Obesity Are Leading to a Diabetes Epidemic

Pepe Escobar

Pepe Escobar is an author and journalist. In the following viewpoint, he connects the obesity crisis in Asian countries with the sharp rise in the diabetes level and states that the specter of "diabesity" (diabetes caused by overweight or obesity) is an albatross around the neck of every country in the region. Escobar notes that a group of experts has come together to treat a neglected aspect of the diabetes crisis, known as the residual vascular risk issue, which the pharmaceutical industry is researching and addressing as well.

As you read, consider the following questions:

1. According to the author, how many people worldwide will be dying of cardiovascular diseases in 2025?
2. How much will diabetes increase in Asia from 2000 to 2025, as noted in the viewpoint?
3. As stated in the viewpoint, what country has the highest number of people with diabetes?

Bangkok—A Big Pharma star player—Sanofi-Aventis—has been battling a stock market tsunami these past few days. It was all caused by a negative rumor about one of its best-

Pepe Escobar, "Superfat Hits Asia," *Asia Times*, July 2, 2009. Reproduced by permission of *Asia Times Online*. www.atimes.com.

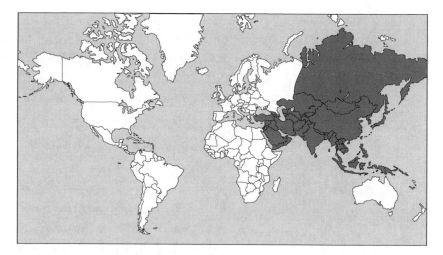

selling products, Lantus (or glargine)—an insulin-a-day wonder that is key in the fight against diabetes.

Tens of thousands of Lantus users panicked. Diabetes is a complex disease with multiple angles, touching tens of millions of people around the world. The stakes—strategic, financial and in terms of health—are enormous. Welcome to the New Health Great Game.

Asia is getting fat. Literally. And that spells trouble. The best specialists agree that obesity is largely responsible for a global diabetes epidemic. For instance, 25% of China's 1.3 billion people are already overweight. 2.8% of Chinese males and 5% of females are obese; and no less than 16.1% of males and 37% of females suffer from what is graciously defined as "abdominal obesity". In a nation of no less than 350 million smokers, 60% of them males, and with female smoking also rising, that spells a monster red alert.

By 2025, no less than 20 million people all over the world will be dying of cardiovascular diseases—mainly coronary diseases and strokes, linked to a cluster of risk factors that include obesity. And this will especially affect low- and middle-income countries, as are most in Asia.

The medical diagnosis is implacable, as presented by Professor Rody Sy, of the University of the Philippines. "Carbohydrates in excess of energy needs" lead to "abdominal obesity", and that causes "dyslipidemia [major alterations in cholesterol traffic], hypertension and diabetes". This carbohydrate-rich diet may be better handled in rural areas, where people move about more often; but in increasingly urbanized—and sedentary—Asia it can be lethal. What to do about it?

In November 2008, in New Orleans, a group of global specialists from North America, Europe and Asia launched the Residual Risk Reduction initiative (known in the industry as R3i). That was packaged as a global program to reduce excess risk of myocardial strokes, kidney diseases, loss of vision and even nontraumatic limb amputation that afflict millions of people with diabetes—even those currently under available medication. R3i has just hit Bangkok, via a conference/workshop designed to spread the wake-up call to doctors from all over Asia.

Statin therapy is the current ABC in the treatment of cholesterol alterations. As specialists describe it, for the past few decades the treatment with statin of vascular risk associated with "lipid disorders" had only dealt with "bad cholesterol". It's time to take on "good cholesterol" as well.

Taxi to the Cholesterol Side

Cholesterol is an essential raw material for cells to work properly. As medical news analyst Dr Jean-Philippe Minart explains it, cholesterol is delivered by an army of "taxis" along a network of highways—the arteries.

Among these taxis, a major transportation company stands out: the LDL cholesterol. They deliver their content to the artery walls. Then scores of trash-carrying trucks come to recover cholesterol from the artery walls, thus preventing their accumulation: These are the HDL cholesterol transporters.

So we have on one side transporters that screw up and make a mess out of it sometimes, the LDL or "bad cholesterol"; and the cleaners, the HDL or "good cholesterol". But this is not about good and evil; the point is that cholesterol should not pile up in the wrong place. It's gotta move all the time.

Coming from our food intake, cholesterol is always in transit. As soon as it's absorbed by our stomach and refined by a factory—our liver—it's transported by the army of taxis along our vessels and to our cells, all of them voracious consumers. If we have too much cholesterol, the number of LDL taxis is higher, cholesterol shoots up and piles up in the artery walls: that's atherosclerosis. Circulation is at risk, and we face a lethal traffic jam—a heart attack.

Statins reduce the circulation of the LDL taxis. In certain cases, more often than not, the trash-carrying trucks may also go on strike. The problem is compounded by the proliferation of an independent taxi enterprise—the TG and the VLDL. These circulation problems have a name: dyslipidemia.

Under these circumstances, the accumulation of cholesterol in the arteries goes on, while we're under the impression the problem has been solved. That's why doctors talk about residual risk, and that's why they want to associate other drugs to statin to act against these disturbing elements. Thus, the task at hand is to lower the number of independent taxis (the TG and VLDL) and increase the number of trash-carrying trucks (HDL). It's much more complicated than it sounds.

Professor Jean Davignon, of the University of Montreal, says the world is "facing a paradigm shift. This is the end of the statin era. We have to look beyond LDL [bad cholesterol]. The broader we are, the better. We must consider all aspects of atherosclerosis". (Atherosclerosis, as mentioned, is the accumulation of cholesterol fat in the arteries.) It was Davignon himself who coined the fabulous term "cholesterocentric world"—

the world we all live in. Now he asks, "But what about other risk factors" causing heart diseases?

Studies show that even with statin treatment, "major coronary events" still happen at a staggering rate of 77%. Moreover, statin and other intensive therapies still cannot prevent the progression of what is called microvascular diseases (which include eye diseases, renal failure and amputation) in up to 50% of patients that already suffer from diabetes. Diabetes and obesity can become evil twins, and are commonly described in the medical industry as "diabesity".

R3i to the Rescue

That's where R3i steps in. Its "mission" is to improve the lives of people suffering from heart disease and/or diabetes. The initiative is adamant: "The residual vascular risk issue has become a major public health challenge in all geographical regions."

This is not philanthropy, of course: The project is run by a Swiss-based foundation, with initial seed funding by Belgian-based Solvay Pharmaceuticals, and led by a board of trustees and an international steering committee of 21 specialists in cardiology, diabetology, lipidology, endocrinology, epidemiology, nutrition, ophthalmology, nephrology and basic science. The foundation is now actively negotiating supplemental grants with other Big Pharma players and the food industry.

According to the *American Journal of Cardiology*, R3i is committed to research, educational programs and making sure that the core issue—technically described as "residual vascular risk associated with atherogenic dyslipidemia"—becomes a global priority. More than 40 countries are already involved in research and educational programs. Professor Sy of the University of the Philippines defines R3i as "a neutral group. What we need to do most of all is to alert primary physicians".

What Is Diabetes?

Diabetes is a disorder of metabolism—the way the body uses digested food for growth and energy. Most of the food people eat is broken down into glucose, the form of sugar in the blood. Glucose is the main source of fuel for the body.

After digestion, glucose passes into the bloodstream, where it is used by cells for growth and energy. For glucose to get into cells, insulin must be present. Insulin is a hormone produced by the pancreas, a large gland behind the stomach.

When people eat, the pancreas automatically produces the right amount of insulin to move glucose from blood into the cells. In people with diabetes, however, the pancreas either produces little or no insulin, or the cells do not respond appropriately to the insulin that is produced. Glucose builds up in the blood, overflows into the urine, and passes out of the body in the urine. Thus, the body loses its main source of fuel even though the blood contains large amounts of glucose.

National Diabetes Information Clearinghouse,
"Diabetes Overview," 2011.

The ghost of "diabesity" is now haunting Asia. From 2000 to 2025, diabetes in Asia will increase by 85%. According to an alarming recent study conducted in 3960 individuals aged 20–74 from urban and rural areas of Fujian, China, 29% were overweight (including 3.5% that were obese). Around 10% suffered from diabetes. And 14.5% had a condition called "impaired glucose tolerance". In a 2002 report on hypertension in China, 24% of individuals were affected, 78% were treating it, but only 19% had it under control.

According to the International Diabetes Federation, in 1985 there were 35 million people with diabetes worldwide; in 2000, there were already 150 million. By 2007, there were more than 110 million in Asia alone. By 2025, there will be a staggering 380 million. In Southeast Asia alone, diabetes among 20- to 79-year-olds, in 2007, affected 46.5 million people. By 2025, it will affect 80.3 million people.

India has the highest number of people with diabetes in the world: 40.9 million. By 2025, also according to the International Diabetes Federation, that number will be 69.9 million. Not to mention an extra 35 million with impaired glucose tolerance.

On a global level, the rate of obesity and overweight children has increased from 0.2% in 1970 to 2% in 2007. This means a staggering 400,000 new cases of obese children every year. It's important to remember that obesity can lead to diabetes.

The Chinese authorities won't fail to notice that the economic burden of diabetes now represents around 17.6 billion yuan (roughly $2.4 billion) a year, and growing.

Welcome to the Lipid War

It goes without saying that R3i is an inevitable by-product of globalization. The directors of the initiative are the first to point out that the road to less residual vascular risk implies weight loss, a healthy diet, frequent exercise and no smoking—even in the case of people already being treated with statin.

But try convincing Asian masses especially in India and China they must abdicate from their Big Mac and fries. Or stop smoking—be it kretek cigarettes in Indonesia, bidis in India or non-filter torpedoes in China. If people won't change, or the appeal of the fast-food industry and the tobacco industry is too powerful, the answer has to come from educating the public plus, inevitably, pharmacotherapy.

R3i recommendations are fundamentally sound. They involve above all a change in lifestyle; normalization of blood pressure; and, as physicians stress, "earlier intervention in the natural history of the disease".

[Try] convincing Asian masses especially in India and China they must abdicate from their Big Mac and fries.

Residual vascular risk is so crucial because research for the past 20 years has identified obesity, dyslipidemia, high blood pressure and raised blood sugar as the key risk factors associated with cardiovascular disease and diabetes. Dyslipidemia alone is a major culprit: 54% as far as the risk of heart attack is concerned.

Microvascular complications, per se, do not kill. But their effects can be simply devastating. For instance, diabetic eye disease is the number one cause of blindness in working-age adults. Diabetic nephropathy is the number one cause of end-stage renal failure. And diabetic neuropathy may lead to amputation of the lower limbs.

For Big Pharma, the so-called Lipid Lowering Agent (LLA) market—the whole business of drugs that lower cholesterol— used to be a booming market ($26 billion in sales in 2008). Now this "gold rush" is over; welcome to the age of generics (mostly made in India).

The fact that the market will inevitably continue to grow in volume also means that the price of the available drugs keeps falling, squeezed by the increased availability of generic drugs. A branded LLA pill costs $3 to $4 a day for the rest of your life. A generic equivalent costs $0.7 to $1.9 a day. The social function of the spread of generics is essential—as they benefit more and more patients.

According to industry data, the LLA market in China in 2008, for instance, was worth almost 1.4 billion yuan (almost US$190 million), with 35 million pills sold. It has been in steady progress since 2004. This reflects a relentless, worldwide growing trend in emerging markets—the new frontier for Big Pharma.

New drugs are expected to be in the market within the next few years. But what kind of drugs? Professor Sy of the Philippines puts it as "a poli-pill. Or various poli-pills, especially helpful for low- to middle-income countries. Single pills that take care of blood pressure, blood sugar, diabetes, will be helpful. But to tackle severe hypertension, several classes of drugs are needed".

The global fast-food industry turns people's eating habits upside down and Big Pharma steps in with a cure.

Yet there's more to it. Once again, why is residual risk so important? Because as mentioned before, people treated with statin are still dying of cardiovascular diseases. Residual risk opens the way to the making of "poli-pills"—in this case, single pills that will tackle all aspects of cholesterol. This means the industry going the crucial step beyond statin. Once again, it's high-stakes poker—a new source of huge profits for Big Pharma, on something that concerns us all, and not only stock market players.

And once again the perverse effects of Asia copying the Western globalization model come full circle. The global fast-food industry turns people's eating habits upside down and Big Pharma steps in with a cure. Everyone profits. But not necessarily those in the wake of their strokes and heart attacks.

Periodical and Internet Sources Bibliography

The following articles have been selected to supplement the diverse views presented in this chapter.

Rosemary Black — "Obesity Is Now the Leading Cause of Cancer," *New York Daily News*, September 24, 2009.

Carole Carson — "The Cost of Obesity," *Huffington Post*, March 7, 2011. www.huffingtonpost.com.

Daniel Engber — "Not Too Fat to Fight," Slate.com, April 23, 2010. www.slate.com.

Lesley Kinzel — "Fat Kids, Cruel World," *Newsweek*, April 20, 2010.

Meredith Melnick — "More Obesity Fallout: Nearly 50 Million Americans with Arthritis," *Time*, October 8, 2010.

Tara Parker-Pope — "An Older Generation Falls Prey to Eating Disorders," *New York Times*, March 28, 2011.

Andrea Pennington — "Childhood Obesity and Diabetes: My Personal Mission," *Huffington Post*, February 2, 2011. www.huffingtonpost.com.

Robert Preidt — "Cost of Obesity Approaching $300 Billion a Year," *USA Today*, January 12, 2011.

Steven Reinberg — "Almost 10 Percent of U.S. Medical Costs Tied to Obesity," ABC News, July 27, 2010. http://abcnews.go.com.

Stephen Robb — "How Obesity Is Reshaping Our World," BBC News, February 3, 2011. www.bbc.co.uk.

Andrea Sachs — "Childhood Obesity and Diabetes: Two Sides of the Same Coin," *Time*, April 27, 2010.

Anti-Obesity Policies

British Politicians Need to Be Thoughtful About Anti-Obesity Policies

Richard Reeves

Richard Reeves is an author and contributor to the New States-man. *In the following viewpoint, he argues that government attempts to address unhealthy behavior, including fat taxes to curb obesity, are paternalistic measures that often infringe on individual freedoms. Reeves contends that British policy makers must decide between interventionist policy measures and respecting individual autonomy.*

As you read, consider the following questions:

1. According to the author, what spurs the politicians' concern over behavior?
2. How does British health minister Alan Johnson think people view the state?
3. How does Reeves describe the role of the market and the state in bringing about behavioral change?

Smoking, smacking, snacking and boozing: Ours is a naughty nation. Billboard advertisements for *St Trinian's*, the UK [United Kingdom] Film Council–funded hymn to anarchy, were covered in the punitive lines: "I must not misbe-

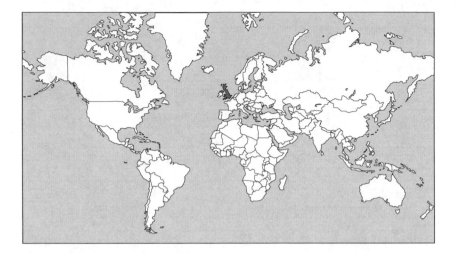

have. I must not misbehave. I must not misbehave." It is not too difficult to imagine the prime minister setting the same lines for the country as a whole. From diets leading to obesity to alcohol-fuelled violence, reducing misbehaviour is now a political priority.

A Trend Toward Intervention

Politicians have historically been wary of appearing to pass judgement on our behaviour, but are becoming more outspoken as the impact of Brits behaving badly is more keenly felt. [Conservative leader] David Cameron has pledged to fix our "broken society", though the chances of a tax break for marriage curbing the behaviour of tanked-up teenagers have to be ranked as thin at best. Early this month [February 2008], the Home Secretary, Jacqui Smith, unveiled plans to give the police powers to seize alcohol from underage drinkers in response to research showing that young people are drinking more heavily—and that alcohol explains a rising proportion of violence among school-age youngsters. Most 13-year-olds surveyed said they have had a drink. "This is a very interesting political space at the moment," says David Halpern, a former government adviser, now at the Institute for Government.

"There is still a fear of being seen to be manipulating people. But [Prime Minister] Gordon Brown has long talked about the need for culture change."

Frank Field, one of the few politicians to speak fearlessly on the issue, has warned of a "new form of barbarism" and "the collapse of decent behaviour" in some of our poorest areas. Even a few years ago, Field sounded eccentrically Victorian. Now there is a chorus of commentators and columnists joining in. Broadsheet op-ed pieces follow a pretty fixed pattern: a first-person account of a shocking incident of antisocial behaviour (usually involving public transport) and next a rash of statistics suggesting that, far from being isolated, it speaks of a wider breakdown of codes of behaviour. Then— depending on the political leanings of the writer—a rant about either the collapse of the traditional family or the rise of rampant individualism. For many decades, an optimistic view of human nature has been in favour on left and right alike; now, the prevailing view is closer to the Hobbesian [after the thinking of English philosopher Thomas Hobbes] one of people's lives being nasty and brutish.

Behaviour leading to obesity is, in strictly liberal terms, beyond the legitimate reach of the state.

Policy Concerns

While personal exposure to some social atrocity is often the spur for members of the commentariat (my own, for what it is worth, involves a van reversing along a pavement outside a school), politicians' concern over behaviour is being driven by clear public policy concerns. Fear of crime hobbles individual freedom; reckless driving kills people; poor diet and lack of exercise cause obesity and necessitate billions in extra NHS [National Health Service] spending; binge drinking drives violence and petty crime. On a less immediate level, a failure to save causes poverty in old age and strain on the public finances. And, of course, meeting the challenge of climate change requires radical alterations in personal behaviour.

But the politics of behavioural change is difficult, at both a philosophical and a practical level. Politicians of all stripes are struggling with the failure of liberal democracy to cope with issues which, in the end, come down to the individual. They are fatally equivocating between two irreconcilable approaches: the paternalist desire to use the levers of the state to enforce better behaviour and the liberal instinct that people should be left alone, unless the actions in question are directly damaging to others. It is a strong liberal principle that activities which harm only the actor should not be interfered with. A gambler blowing his life savings at the baccarat table may be as foolish as the bank robber, but the foolishness of the former hurts only himself.

Behaviour leading to obesity is, in strictly liberal terms, beyond the legitimate reach of the state. If I eat badly and live as a couch potato, the only person who will get fat is me. That is why it is ludicrous to talk of an "obesity epidemic". It is hard to imagine genuine liberals such as the late Roy Jenkins getting worked up about weight gain. Nonetheless, the profound impact of obesity on health—some studies suggest obesity knocks a decade off life expectancy—has led to lots of political rhetoric on the issue.

The Challenge of Changing Individual Behaviours

Alan Johnson, the Health Secretary, who (absurdly) compares obesity to global warming, judges that people are just as opposed to a "neglectful state" as a "nanny state". Various small-budget, "cross-cutting" initiatives have been launched, and a few policies trailed—from changing planning laws to make it harder to open a fast-food outlet to compulsory school weigh-ins and warning letters to parents of chubby children. But the government has shied away from bolder options, such as a tax on fatty foods, or even a compulsory "traffic light" system to make it easier for shoppers to spot waist-threatening items.

Antisocial behaviour offers a clearer rationale for state intervention. Noise, public disorder and threatening behaviour are all harmful to others: The "neighbours from hell" really can make life hell. The truth is that only communities themselves can effectively regulate the low-level misbehaviour of their members—the state is too distant. As such, antisocial behaviour orders (Asbos) have a mixed record; in many areas an Asbo has become a badge of honour rather than shame. As the late Linda Smith put it: "Don't knock Asbos—for some of these kids it's the only qualification they'll get."

One of the frustrations for policy makers is that many of the problems associated with individual behaviour are, by definition, beyond the reach of legislation. Only the most draconian laws could have any discernible impact on the problems of obesity, antisocial behaviour or alcohol abuse. [British author and moralist] Samuel Johnson knew this: "How small, of all that human hearts endure/That part which Laws or Kings can cause or cure."

The field of behavioural psychology has been supplemented by the burgeoning discipline of behavioural economics—but we are a very long way from a science of behavourial politics.

Manipulation

One ray of hope comes from evidence that patterns of behaviour can be changed quite significantly, especially in response to changes in surrounding environment. "When you suggest quite small policy changes, people make the accusation that you're just tinkering," says Halpern. "But in fact quite small changes can have quite big effects." A story from the US scholar Robert Cialdini's *Influence: Science and Practice*—a bible for behaviourists—showed how a restaurant reduced the rate of people failing to turn up for a table booking from 30

Obesity in England

- In 2009, almost a quarter of adults (22% of men and 24% of women aged 16 or over) in England were classified as obese. . . .

- A greater proportion of men than women (44% compared with 33%) in England were classified as overweight in 2009. . . .

- Thirty-eight per cent of adults had a raised waist circumference in 2009 compared to 23% in 1993. Women were more likely than men (44% and 32% respectively) to have a raised waist circumference. . . .

- Using both BMI [body mass index] and waist circumference to assess risk of health problems, for men: 19% were estimated to be at increased risk; 14% at high risk and 20% at very high risk in 2009. Equivalent figures for women were: 14% at increased risk, 18% at high risk and 23% at very high risk.

- In 2009, around three in ten boys and girls aged 2 to 15 were classed as either overweight or obese (31% and 28% respectively), which is very similar to the 2008 findings (31% for boys and 29% for girls).

- In 2009, 16% of boys aged 2 to 15, and 15% of girls were classed as obese, an increase from 11% and 12% respectively in 1995. . . .

National Health Service,
"Statistics on Obesity, Physical Activity and Diet:
England, 2011," 2011.

to 10 per cent by making an apparently tiny change to the conversation when a table was booked. Staff had always said something like: "Please let us know if you can't come." Now they were asked to say: "You will let us know if you can't come, won't you?" and then—crucially—pause and wait for a response. The answer sealed a kind of contract.

Is this a form of psychological manipulation? Cialdini argues that far from being manipulative, such techniques are simply about better communication (though there is something creepy about the deliberateness of the ploy). What relevance does the number of no-shows at a restaurant in California have for British public policy? One in ten of us has failed to show up for a GP [medical doctor] appointment and "failures to attend" cost the NHS £325m[illion] a year. Rather than fines (a policy occasionally considered), perhaps there is some way to increase the "contract" of the appointment.

It is not just Labour's policy wonks who are into behaviour. On the Conservative side, David Willetts is looking at game theory to see how institutional settings can encourage or discourage co-operative behaviour (while Lord Tebbit has been trumpeting his own solution for young black Britons trapped in a culture of gangs, guns and drugs: "a good game of rugger").

What Willetts and Halpern share is an appreciation of the environmental influence on individual behaviour. We don't make our decisions in a vacuum; they are hugely shaped by a range of factors, including mood and peer influence. There is now a considerable body of research literature showing that people's level of social helpfulness is more influenced by how they feel at a particular point in time than by their personality. In the most famous staged experiment, people were considerably more likely to help a stranger pick up the papers she had dropped if they themselves had been "lucky" enough to find a dime in the pay phone they had just used. Out of 15 who got the extra dime, 14 helped the woman with her papers; of the 26 who did not, only two did. There are countless other examples of what might be labelled mood multiplier effect: someone who is offered a courtesy on the road is more likely to do the same for someone else, for example. Kindness seems to be contagious. This of course means that unkindness, too, is likely to be self-perpetuating.

Going round dropping pound coins in odd places would be a fun government job, and there would surely be a few candidates for minister of moodiness: but there is little the government can—or, indeed, should—do to improve our mood. A potentially more fruitful way into behaviour change is the influence of peers and communities. Social behaviour displays what David Hirshleifer, a professor at Ohio State University's business school, calls "localised conformity".

The human tendency to imitate is powerful; it makes both good and bad behaviour become normalised and hard to turn around. This also applies to appearance: people with a friend who becomes overweight are more likely to become overweight themselves.

Affecting Behavioural Change

The human tendency to imitate is powerful; it makes both good and bad behaviour become normalised and hard to turn around. This also applies to appearance: people with a friend who becomes overweight are more likely to become overweight themselves, and judgements about what constitutes a "normal" body shape are changing almost as quickly as body shapes themselves, one reason why the parents of clinically obese children sometimes deny it.

The political right is correct to suggest that self-regulation—or character—is vital. A good society cannot be built without good people. But the left accurately identifies the role of collective life, and of institutions, in the shaping of behaviour. What both need to come to terms with is the impotence of the market *and* the state in bringing about behavioural change.

Killer Question

The positions of government and opposition alike are riddled with inconsistency. Both are stuck between the rock of paternalism and the hard place of liberalism. The killer question, which is being universally ducked, is how far the state can or should save us from ourselves.

Labour's approach to obesity offers perhaps the best example. Alan Johnson has two intellectually respectable options. He could argue that the state must intervene dramatically on obesity and stop fiddling around with "cross-government initiatives". He should slap a tax on bad food and ban corporations from advertising junk food to children—a piece of paternalism that few except the firms themselves could oppose. Failing this, he needs to admit that individually caused obesity is not an issue a government in a liberal society can do very much about.

Johnson—as do politicians generally—needs to decide whether to be a good paternalist or a good liberal, rather than encourage the present awful hybrid of ineffective paternalism and false liberalism. Every parent knows that making threatening noises but failing to follow up with action is a recipe for domestic anarchy. The same is true of the state. The government does have a choice: do something, or shut up.

Germany Examines Food Labeling Programs to Curb Obesity

Michaela Schiessl and Markus Verbeet

Michaela Schiessl and Markus Verbeet are journalists. In the following viewpoint, they discuss the debate over Germany's proposed mandatory labeling system, which is based on England's traffic light system that uses color-coded labels to identify high-fat and sugary foods. Schiessl and Verbeet report that the policy has come under fire from the food industry lobby and consumer protection advocates.

As you read, consider the following questions:

1. According to the authors, what percentage of Germans are considered obese?

2. Why are portion sizes a controversial aspect of the old, voluntary labeling system in Germany, according to the authors?

3. As stated in the viewpoint, what is the Brussels plan for mandatory food labeling for the European Union?

Few in Germany's parliament expected the kind of heated debate that would be sparked when it began to discuss the issue of food labeling last month [March 2008]. But industry,

Michaela Schiessl and Markus Verbeet, "Germany Mulls Mandatory Food Labels," *Der Spiegel*, April 17, 2008. Reproduced by permission.

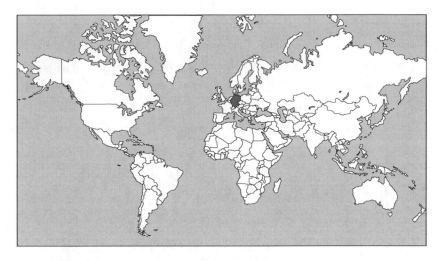

politicians and consumer protection advocates have long been waging a bitter battle over food labeling practices. Some are concerned about their business, while others are worried about consumer health and the costs to society at large.

More than half of Germans are overweight, and 20 percent are considered obese. Almost 2 million children and adolescents are too fat. Thirty percent of the costs within the German healthcare system—more than €70 billion a year, and a number that is rising—are attributable to the consequences of food-related illnesses. The World Health Organization (WHO) calls it an epidemic.

All parties agree that better food labeling could help guide consumers through a jungle of an estimated 240,000 products available on the German market. More importantly, it could help them to differentiate between healthy and unhealthy foods, and whether what they are putting in their shopping cart is a calorie bomb or not. Most agree that if a system is put in place it must also be easy to understand, since overweight people tend to belong to social classes with lower education levels. But what should this food road map look like?

The Traffic Light System

The Green Party, the Left Party, and now the Social Democrats (SPD), wanted to join forces with consumer groups to implement the type of color-coded system, known as the traffic light, already in use in Great Britain. The British system includes color-coded labels on products with fats, sugar and salt according to their relative amounts—red for foods that are too much of a bad thing, yellow for borderline goods and green for those that can be eaten without worry.

All parties agree that better food labeling could help guide consumers through a jungle of an estimated 240,000 products available on the German market.

Opposition to the Proposal

But the food industry lobby calls this "discrimination against products," as if brand names had human rights, and it has managed to win over Horst Seehofer, the country's minister of food, agriculture and consumer protection. The traffic light system, says Seehofer, represents a "brainwashing of the people," while the food manufacturers' proposal is more objective and less patronizing.

In fact, the traffic light system would be devastating for the dessert products industry, because most of its goods would be labeled a deep red. Instead, Seehofer is backing an industry proposal to provide individual values for nutrients and express them as a percentage of the recommended daily requirement. Calories would be listed on a product's front label while other information would be shown on the back. Of course, all of this would be voluntary.

Seehofer, together with food industry officials, presented the key elements of this so-called GDA model in October, and later injected them into the European debate.

Political Maneuvering

The whole thing looked like a fait accompli [done deal] for the food industry lobby. But then Gerd Müller, a state secretary in Seehofer's consumer protection ministry with the conservative Christian Social Union (CSU) party, showed up at the March 6 debate in the German parliament.

In his speech, Müller said, almost as an aside, something that was considered unmentionable until then: "To your surprise, we plan to test a labeling system in which red, yellow and green play a role. We launched a survey to this effect yesterday." The table on Müller's handout had a red, yellow and green background. Politicians within Müller's CSU and its larger sister party, the Christian Democratic Union (CDU), could hardly believe their eyes. There was something unmistakably traffic-lightish about the document.

Since then, people representing all sides of the debate have been left scratching their heads over whether Seehofer, a man known for his ability to sense the general mood, has switched sides now that resistance to the industry plans has grown and politicians have realized that the food labeling controversy could become a campaign issue.

Political Blowback

Thilo Bode, director of the German consumer protection organization Foodwatch, tirelessly criticizes the policies of the consumer affairs minister on the radio and on television, as well as in his book *Abgespeist* (*Fobbed Off*). "With his rejection of the traffic light system, Horst Seehofer has made himself the chief lobbyist for the food industry. He has failed in the one area where he could really take significant steps to combat the problem of obesity: clear and understandable product labeling."

Bode refuses to give credence to the argument that the traffic light system is too simple and paints a distorted and negative image of products that are in fact good (think of margarine and olive oil). "People are fed up with having to decipher unclear rows of figures in small print on package labels."

Foodwatch supporters have sent more than 10,000 e-mails objecting to the traffic light system to the consumer affairs ministry. A new major digital offensive has also been under way since last week, and residents of Germany can now tell their elected representatives what they think by logging on to a special Web site.

A Successful Program in Britain

The biggest and most influential proponents of the traffic light system are Germany's consumer protection agencies. Experts there feel experiences in Great Britain show that consumers like and understand the labels. "There is nothing patronizing about this," says Stefan Etgeton of the federal association of consumer protection. "It is an urgently needed shopping tool."

His colleagues at the consumer protection agency in Hamburg reinforced their pro–traffic light position in a recently published and eye-opening study. It examines how the industry uses arbitrary lists of ingredients to fudge its way into making food products appear healthy. To make nutritional value figures seem as appealing as possible, portion sizes are listed on labels that have very little to do with the reality of an evening spent at home on the couch. For example, the nutritional values on a package of peanuts are given for a portion size of 25 grams—a small share of what is actually in the bag. The same applies to potato chips. The savvy consumer, if he hopes to remain within the calorie limits printed on labels, is expected to make do with a portion of four little chocolates and then close the box and put it away, or to drink only half of a half-liter bottle of Coca-Cola or eat half of a frozen pizza.

These cheap tricks harm the industry's credibility. And although 60 percent of products are already labeled voluntarily, as long as there is no uniform labeling system, the information that is currently being provided is more likely to obfuscate than reveal.

The biggest and most influential proponents of the traffic light system are Germany's consumer protection agencies.

Peb & Pebber

No amount of government intervention into social policy, such as the "Nutrition and Exercise Platform" promoted by the German government, can change this. As members of the initiative, Nestlé and Danone support a television program created specifically to serve its needs, *Peb & Pebber*. In the program, which will be aired on the children's channel Super RTL, two hand puppets will introduce healthy nutrition to children. But the ads airing during the program do just the opposite, tempting children with Danone's Fruchtzwerge dairy dessert, the yoghurt drink Actimel and Nestlé's Cini Minis breakfast cereal.

All three products are loaded with calories. Fruchtzwerge, a product containing fromage frais, contains 14.4 grams of carbohydrates, almost all sugar, for each 100 grams. Normal fromage frais contains only 3.1 grams of carbohydrates. Actimel, a yoghurt drink, contains 10.5 grams of sugar, compared to only 4.1 grams in normal low-fat yoghurt. Nestlé's breakfast snack, Cini Minis, has almost as many calories as chocolate. Of every 100 grams, 32.8 are pure sugar.

What is this sort of advertising doing in a children's program that promotes good nutrition? "Children should learn to eat a balanced diet, and to consume everything in moderation," says Nestlé spokesman Hartmut Gahmann. Besides, he adds, children would burn more calories if they only exercised more.

A few days after the interview, the company sends out an e-mail notice stating that it has cancelled its ad campaign for Cini Minis in the *Peb & Pebber* program as of March 2008. "There are no plans to reintroduce this advertising in this program." Besides, the memo notes, the product's sugar content was reduced in the past two years by about 12 percent, to its current value of 32.8 grams per 100 grams of cereal. "We will continue this reduction process," Nestlé writes.

Skepticism of Voluntary Labeling

Consumer protection advocates also hold a skeptical view of the industry's new food labeling model. They object to the inconsistent portion sizes and the "allowable daily value" category, which is based on the requirements of an adult woman. But children and the elderly require significantly less energy, while men and people in physically demanding occupations require more. Thus, it comes as no surprise that doctors are also speaking out in favor of the far more straightforward color-coding system.

Gerd Claussnitzer, who, as physician-in-chief of the Spessart Hospital in the central German town of Bad Orb, treats overweight children, believes that the traffic light system can be useful. "Color coding—be it through a traffic light symbol or the less judgmental food pyramid—is easier to understand, especially for children." The system would help prevent obesity, says Claussnitzer, because "many children's foods would come with a red dot."

The food industry is also running up against Germany's largest health insurance association. "Consumers need a simple and clear system that allows them to recognize whether a food product contains too much fat, sugar or salt. The traffic light solution, which has tested well in England, offers precisely these characteristics, especially because it includes both color coding and precise amounts," says Hans Jürgen Ahrens, the chairman of German's largest health insurer, AOK-

Bundesverband. "If German waist sizes are to be brought down once again, it's important for consumers to be able to tell, directly on supermarket shelves, whether they are buying healthy or high-fat foods."

Testing the Traffic Light System

With his surprising about-face in favor of testing a color-coded system, Seehofer is distancing himself from his strict opposition to the idea for the first time. "We want to test how consumers perceive the GDA model if it is combined with red-green-yellow," admits Ursula Heinen of the CDU, who is a parliamentary state secretary in Seehofer's ministry. The survey was completed on March 31, but the results have not been analyzed yet, says Heinen.

But what happens if people like the color-coded system? "We will not act without taking the needs of consumers into account," says Heinen. But concessions to industry will be necessary, she adds. What those concessions could look like remains vague, however.

Strategy of the Food Industry

The industry, for its part, seems disappointed. "We would like to see more clarity. After all, Seehofer was consistently opposed to the traffic light system until now. And yet, what they're now testing is a traffic light system," says Matthias Horst, managing director of the German Federation for Food Law and Food Science (BLL), the lobbying organization for the food industry.

The industry was confident until now. Representatives of major food corporations, like Nestlé, Unilever and Kellogg's, have been meeting regularly since 2004 to develop strategies. They hired PR [public relations] agencies to design campaigns against the British color-coded system and assiduously lobbied the European Commission in Brussels. Their associations maintained close contact with the German consumer protection ministry—apparently with great success, or so it seemed.

"Surgeon General's warning on junk food! Lighten up a little!," cartoon by Jack Corbett, www.CartoonStock.com. Copyright © Jack Corbett. Reproduction rights obtainable from www.CartoonStock.com.

At first, Seehofer accepted the BLL model at face value, promising to preserve the voluntary nature of food labeling.

The Brussels Plan

The first setback for the industry came in late January, when Brussels presented its own proposal for food labeling across the European Union [EU]. Under the Brussels plan, all food packages will list calories, fat content, carbohydrates, sugar, salt and saturated fatty acids on the front label. The back label would then provide information on recommended daily allowances of individual ingredients, and what percentage of those allowances the product contains. Even the font size is regulated under the EU proposal, which stipulates that words must be at least three millimeters tall.

Markos Kyprianou, the EU health commissioner in office during development of the proposal, took it a step further than the German model, which calls for listing calories on the front label and everything else on the back. But what is far more important about the EU plan is that labeling would be mandatory. This came as a shock to the food industry, and yet it celebrated its own victory of sorts: The European plan takes the traffic light concept off the table for now.

"We want informed consumers, but we don't want to make their decisions for them," Kyprianou said, thereby delegating the decision to each individual member state. The EU plan leaves it up to each country to introduce its own version of the "traffic light." But this presents the EU with exactly the kind of situation it was trying to avoid with its internal market: regulations that differ in each country. And for the industry it is nothing short of a horrific scenario that would only lead to "more confusion instead of information for consumers," the Confederation of the Food and Drink Industries of the European Union (CIAA) argues.

Moving Forward

Now it is time for the European Parliament and member states to reach a decision on the European Commission's proposal. This could take some time; leaders of the EU member states have only met for an initial meeting to discuss the issue, and many in the EU parliament are skeptical that an agreement can be reached before the next European elections in June 2009.

Officials in Seehofer's ministry, on the other hand, have a more positive take on the matter and expect a quick decision before the elections. Until then, the officials say, Germany will not try to go it alone.

Does this signify the demise of the traffic light system once and for all, or the last reprieve for the industry model? Gerd Müller's next appearance is keenly anticipated.

Canada Does Not Have the Political Will to Implement Broad Anti-Obesity Measures

Ken MacQueen

Ken MacQueen is a reporter for Maclean's. *In the following viewpoint, he bemoans the lack of political will in Canada to post calorie counts for fast food that could be a valuable measure in the fight against the growing obesity crisis in Canada. Mac-Queen identifies a restaurant lobbying group, the Canadian Restaurant and Foodservices Association, to be a significant obstacle in passing a calorie-posting law.*

As you read, consider the following questions:

1. As stated in the viewpoint, what American baseball team started posting the calorie count of all food sold at its stadium?
2. What Canadian official recommended a calorie-counting measure to the Canadian government, according to the viewpoint?
3. Why does Ron Reaman claim that calorie counting isn't needed in Canada?

B aseball is a numbers game, and few teams produce more impressive stats than the New York Yankees. Their new stadium opened in 2009 and promptly delivered the team's

Ken MacQueen, "Calories Made Visible," *Maclean's*, June 4, 2010. Reproduced by permission.

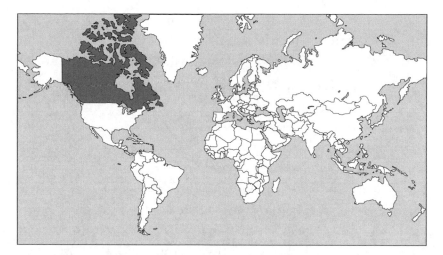

27th World Series win. To stroll amid the sights and smells of the food vendors is to see another legacy at play, one that will linger for a lifetime in the hearts of Yankee fans.

Nathan's Famous foot-long beef hot dog clocks in at 500 calories before condiments. That's one-quarter of the roughly 2,000 calories you need in a day. At Moe's, the "nachos supreme" set you back 1,410 calories. Elsewhere, a jumbo popcorn is 1,484 calories, and the souvenir bucket is 2,473. Add a couple of beers (286 calories for a large Beck's) and you see why, when the Yanks moved from their circa-1920s stadium, they widened the seats by as much as two inches.

In the Big Apple you know in a New York minute what your food costs—in dollars *and* in calories. Both numbers have equal prominence on the menus and menu boards of the city's chain restaurants—by order of the New York Department of Health and Mental Hygiene. It's an attempt to stem a frightening increase in obesity, an epidemic also killing Canadians and compromising the health care system. Unlike in Canada, there is political will in the U.S. to take action. By next spring, the Obama administration's sweeping health care reform bill requires U.S. restaurant chains to post calorie counts on menu boards, drive-throughs and vending machines. It was one of the few non-contentious parts of the bill—a recognition by legislators, and the American restaurant industry, of an anti-obesity measure whose time has come.

Not so in Canada. Don't expect to find a quick, easy calorie count on either the restaurant or national political menu anytime soon—despite what the Public Health Agency of Canada calls "an alarming increase" in obesity and attendant health problems. And even though measures similar to the U.S. law are endorsed by the Dietitians of Canada, the Centre for Science in the Public Interest, the Ontario Medical Association, by weight-loss specialists, by the B.C. government and by Dr. Kellie Leitch, a federal adviser on healthy children and youth.

Don't expect to find a quick, easy calorie count on either the restaurant or national political menu anytime soon—despite what the Public Health Agency of Canada calls "an alarming increase" in obesity and attendant health problems.

Leitch's 2008 report, *Reaching for the Top*, dealt extensively with overweight youth. The prominent display of calories at restaurants was among her recommendations to then health minister Tony Clement. As a pediatric orthopaedic surgeon she sees in her own clinic a "frightening" increase in type 2 diabetes among adolescents, the result of poor diet, little exercise and excess calories. "We will have a generation of children that is projected to not live as long as their parents," she told *Maclean's*. She expects the government to eventually act on some of her obesity recommendations but so far she's heard nothing.

Lobbying against a calorie law is the well-connected Canadian Restaurant and Foodservices Association (CRFA), which purports to know better. Singling out calories "doesn't meet

Growing Obesity in the United States and Canada

Between the late 1980s and today, the prevalence of obesity increased significantly in both the United States and Canada. In Canadian men the prevalence rose by approximately 10 percentage points and among men in the United States, the prevalence rose by 12 percentage points. Among women, the increase was approximately 8 percentage points in Canada and approximately 10 percentage points in the United States.

Over the 20-year period, patterns of increase were fairly consistent across age groups in both the United States and Canada. Among men, the increase was highest among those aged 60 to 74. In this age group, obesity increased 17 percentage points in Canada and approximately 18 percentage points in the United States. Among women, the increases were highest among those aged 20 to 39.

In 2007 to 2009, the prevalence of obesity among young and middle-aged Canadian women (aged 20 to 59) was similar to or lower than that observed in U.S. women 20 years earlier.

Statistics Canada,
"Adult Obesity Prevalence in Canada and the United States," 2011.

the needs of our customers," says Ron Reaman, a vice-president with the CRFA. "Our customers have a wide array of dietary concerns." Limiting the menu information to calories wouldn't help those worried about things like carbohydrates, sodium or trans fat, he says: "Never mind allergies." You can't put all that on the menu, the thinking goes, so none of it belongs.

Instead, the association has a voluntary "nutrition information program." Some 33 participating restaurant chains provide an array of nutritional information in varying formats and degrees of visibility. Most have extensive information on company websites; others have brochures or, in the case of McDonald's, descriptions in exhaustive detail on the back of tray liners. "We believe that this is a responsible approach that responds to the needs of our customers," says Reaman. "We think it is actually a better approach than what they're doing in the U.S."

"Ron's full of it, but that's his job," says Dr. Yoni Freedhoff, founder of Ottawa's Bariatric Medical Institute, which specializes in nonsurgical weight management. "It's a ridiculous assertion to suggest that people are looking for [all] that information," says Freedhoff, also the author of the lively obesity website weightymatters.ca. "When we go shopping for things we look at price tags before we buy them so we can determine whether they're worth it to us," he says. "When we eat things, the currency of our weight is calories." Certainly estimating calories isn't always intuitive.

Even without checking Kelsey's restaurant website you might guess their fully loaded nachos (at 2,160 calories that's a day's worth of eating) had best be shared. But would you think a chicken quesadilla and accompanying rice top out at 1,130 calories? Or that, at Casey's Bar & Grill, a vegetarian pad Thai is 740 calories, a side of sweet potato fries is 760, but an order of one-piece fish and regular chips is just 330 calories?

Indonesia Addresses the Complex Problem of Obesity

Keith Hargreaves

Keith Hargreaves is a director at Strategic Asia Indonesia. In the following viewpoint, he identifies obesity and smoking as examples of "wicked problems," or a series of interconnected and multidimensional problems. Hargreaves describes wicked problems as ones that are difficult to address and require the cooperation of many agencies and policy makers to coordinate solutions on a number of levels.

As you read, consider the following questions:

1. According to the author, what should be the first step in addressing obesity?
2. What does Hargreaves say about the role of industrialization in Indonesia's growing obesity crisis?
3. Does Hargreaves agree with Britain including fast-food producers as advisors on health policy?

Policies are only fit for purpose if they target the right problem. But what if a problem is not really "one problem" but a series of connected problems? Issues relating to democratic change, human rights and health reform, for example, often come under this category. An Australian government publication described these types of multidimensional

Keith Hargreaves, "Strategic Asia: Wicked Solutions to Wicked Problems?" *Jakarta Globe*, December 21, 2010. Reproduced by permission.

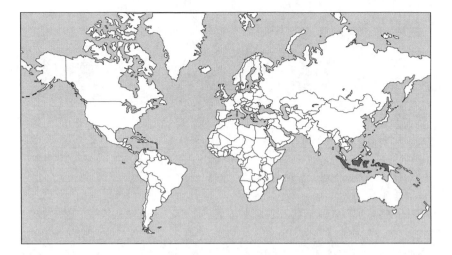

issues as "wicked problems": too complicated for one policy, one agency or one approach to tackle.

Two Wicked Problems

Two such problems regularly in the news are overeating and smoking. What can we learn from how policy makers approach them?

The first step is deciding where the "problem" lies. Obesity is blamed on a variety of factors. To name but some: an over-zealous media trying to sell fatty and unhealthy food; our tendency to inertia over movement (we are lazy at heart); a change in work and home environments where we can indulge our propensity to inertia; the development of a snack culture where fast food is sold as more convenient, better and tastier than food that needs time to cook, to savor and to share.

As the problem of obesity spreads around the globe, many have blamed globalization. One look at children in any of Jakarta's malls can tell you that obesity is becoming an issue in some strata of society in Indonesia. Certainly it is globalization that brought many of the problems to our supermarket shelves but it is parents who put these products on our tables. It is skilled advertisers who tell us these products have charm, or are cool, or even that we need them, but it is parents who buy them. Is globalization, advertising, laziness, an overattentive parent or a spoiled child thus the "real" issue? Or is it a combination of all?

As the problem of obesity spreads around the globe, many have blamed globalization.

A Complicated Issue

Imagine you were charged with drawing up policy to tackle the growing number of overweight children in Jakarta. Where would you begin? Governments have written policies encouraging exercise as a way of shedding pounds. Children like watching TV or playing video games. Health messages are reinforcing the connection between overweight kids growing into overweight adults and health problems that overweight adulthood can bring, such as diabetes and heart disease.

Would a policy encouraging advertisers to promote products more matter-of-factly work? Would ensuring consumers know just how much salt, fat or other unhealthy substances are in their food reduce consumption? One suspects not. Would children not want them if they knew more about what they contain? It tastes good, so one suspects not. Would banning junk food altogether work? One suspects not.

The right to eat what we like and the reality that many imported foods are a good source of tax revenue complicates this obvious choice, at least for the government and financiers.

Smoking

Smoking is a similar issue, one that for many has an obvious solution: ban it. But what is the "it" that should be banned? Smoking, smokers or the smoke they puff out? The answer depends on which authority you ask.

The Ministry of Health is unequivocal. Smoking is danger-ous to everyone's health and it should be eliminated. This would reduce the number of early deaths of smokers, the number of people dying from secondhand smoke, the burden on the health care system, bad breath and those tiny kretek holes in what were perfectly good shirts before smokers pocked them.

Officials of Jakarta Governor Fauzi Bowo's administration have a slightly different take: banning smoking in public areas. I am for it, but even as a rabid anti-smoker, I want to talk to my wayward smoking friends now and then. It is not smokers I want to ban, it is their smoke.

Finding a Solution

Smokers argue for their right to smoke. They have a point. But I also believe I have a right to breathe fresh air. Thus is the issue here smokers, their right to smoke or the smoke they produce, which in turn harms my right to clean air? As virtu-ally no one heeds the ban in cafes and bars, smokers vote with their lighters.

Another reason why banning smoking in public areas is not working is that cafe workers won't enforce the restriction because smokers are the majority of their customers. Empty seats do not make money. Thus if the policy does not work, is there a policy that would benefit more stakeholders?

Why not let all establishments who want to allow smoking in their establishments do so, but insist they install extractors that suck up smoke so it does not bother others? Why not tax them more for this privilege? Why not give tax breaks to those cafes that enforce the ban on smoking, thus rewarding "the healthy choice."

A Compromise?

Who would benefit?

I would for sure. I would have a choice of a completely smoke-free environment, guaranteed, with cheaper coffee as owners could charge less, given the tax breaks they have. I could occasionally sit in a smokers' cafe and talk to friends but not be bothered by their habit. The owners would still have a thriving business. Jakarta authorities would have increased tax revenues.

Who would lose out? The Ministry of Health would see anything but a total ban as a compromise. But perhaps it would be happy with the interim measure. Cigarette companies would see their sales maintained and, in the biggest irony of all, the Jakarta authorities would maintain high revenues from taxes on cigarettes and companies that make them.

Important Factors

The difficulties facing policy decisions in relation to these two wicked problems are clear. Furthermore there are some overarching issues and reality checks that need to be factored in when deciding on policy content. The growing demand for a full set of human rights cannot be ignored; democracies need taxes as governments have limited budgets; people make their own choices about what goes into their mouths; behavior is difficult to change.

Whatever your stance on overeating and smoking, wicked problems cause policy makers many a sleepless night.

And instruments that generate new policy, such as the British system of White Papers, often take years to be compiled because there are so many stakeholders to consult. As a result these methods are very expensive and many governments do not use them, preferring to limit the number of stakeholders they consult. Finally, it is not just about the number of stakeholders but how representative they are. An editorial this month [December 2010] in the *Guardian Weekly* highlighted Britain's inclusion of fast-food producers as advisers on health policy. Not all health sector policy makers in

Britain were happy with what to them seems like a conflict of interest. Can fast-food producers be impartial in a debate on a policy in which they are frequently seen as the villains? Policies must not be captured by vested interests.

Whatever your stance on overeating and smoking, wicked problems cause policy makers many a sleepless night. But somebody has to do it. Just be thankful you have delegated others to do the job on your behalf.

US Policy Makers Consider New Taxes and Regulations on Certain Foods

Richard Conniff

Richard Conniff is a nonfiction writer. In the following viewpoint, he maintains that the US obesity crisis is caused not only by a lack of personal responsibility and willpower, but by an "obesogenic" environment, which he describes as a world that makes it too easy for individuals to get fat. Conniff describes some measures that policy makers are considering to counter this environment, including taxes on junk food, limiting the advertising of fast food to children, and creating a pro-exercise environment for adults and kids.

As you read, consider the following questions:

1. What percentage of Americans are overweight or obese, as stated in the viewpoint?

2. According to the viewpoint, what percentage of school-age children in the United States suffer from childhood obesity?

3. As described in the viewpoint, how much sugar a year does the average American consume?

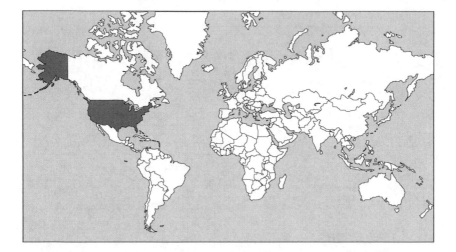

At an all-you-can-eat Italian buffet in upstate New York, the feature attraction is *abbondanza*—an abundance of lasagna, ziti, chicken wings, shrimp, salads, soft drinks, and dozens of pizza varieties, including one topped with bananas, cinnamon, and soft ice cream.

The patrons display a certain *abbondanza*, too, as they huddle at their tables. Many of them look bearlike—a slug of flesh around the backs of their necks, and their legs spread to cradle the body part known in slang as the FUPA, or fatty upper pelvic (or cruder term) area. The ceiling lights up with digital fireworks. But the patrons hardly notice as they struggle to their feet and shuffle to the buffet for another round.

An "Obesogenic" Environment

I don't hate these people, despite the title I gave my article in last month's *Men's Health* [October 2010]—"I Hate Fat People." I've come to realize that our surroundings, our society, and even our economic system have created a world that makes it too easy for people to become fat. Perhaps all the blame doesn't belong on those patrons' rounded shoulders.

One of the diners, a lean, 50-year-old Cornell University professor named Brian Wansink, Ph.D., prudently chooses a small plate. Wansink, who studies eating behavior, says we make more than 200 such minor food decisions every day, mostly without thinking. (Hence his book *Mindless Eating.*) One of his studies found, for instance, that heavier customers at just this sort of buffet tend to take large plates instead of small ones, serve themselves immediately instead of checking out the food first, and sit facing the buffet at an open table, not in a booth. (And men, according to a study of dating couples, often think that eating big is a sign of being manly, studly, or even insatiable.)

We live in what some experts describe as an "obesogenic" environment—a world geared to make us fat.

And yet Wansink piles his plate with high-calorie stuff, topped, as a sort of farewell kiss to prudence, with a low-cal salad dressing. Later he goes back for seconds, plus two slices of pizza. Full disclosure: That banana ice cream pizza? It's mine. This buffet is just too much to resist—a couple of days' worth of calories for a price, $12 a head, that's less than a couple of hours' pay, even at minimum wage.

And right there you have the sweet downfall of life in the modern age—and perhaps the key to global obesity. We live in what some experts describe as an "obesogenic" environment—a world geared to make us fat. Food is ridiculously cheap. Where feeding ourselves cost about 20 percent of household income in 1960, we spend less than 12 percent today, including what we spend on eating out and groceries. Moreover, it's the wrong food that's become most economical (particularly high-calorie fats, oils, and sugars), not fresh fruits and vegetables.

At the same time, physical labor has largely vanished from our lives. Manufacturing is down from a quarter of all jobs in 1970 to less than 10 percent today. Agriculture shrank from 40 percent of jobs in 1900 to less than 2 percent in 2000. Our ancestors earned their daily bread by the sweat of their brows. We earn our daily doughnuts by pushing buttons on keyboards.

The US Obesity Crisis

It would be heaven, if it weren't killing us: Two-thirds of Americans are now overweight or obese; this resulted in an extra $147 billion in health care costs in 2008 alone. A third of men and 40 percent of women born in this century in the United States will become diabetic, experts say, meaning they'll probably die debilitated and before their time. After tobacco, being overweight is the second leading preventable cause of cancer.

In the great debate over what to do about it, the "personal responsibility" camp says the remedy lies in changing our own behaviors. The obesogenic-environment crowd says we can no longer do it by ourselves. Marketing tactics and the abundance of cheap, energy-dense snacks and beverages have conspired for decades to make us sick, they contend, and that's where the big changes need to happen.

It is at times a strange debate, with once-wholesome food companies now often classed with tobacco merchants as purveyors of unhealthy products skillfully targeted to boost demand. Major food corporations, threatened with fat taxes and tighter regulation, have become ardent advocates of exercise and consumer education. This sometimes puts health advocates in the odd position of arguing that exercise is not the main answer to the obesity epidemic.

The Role of Personal Responsibility

But let's start with the personal responsibility side. An old friend, a former competitive swimmer gone to fat, is in the hospital having his hip replaced. Another friend spent the other day at the hospital helping her husband prepare for a coronary bypass. For lunch a few days before the surgery, the man, who is diabetic, ate a doughnut à la mode, much like a lung cancer patient who smokes a cigarette on his way to chemotherapy. Their son, who is in his early 30s, does not understand why he already has high blood pressure.

I don't mean to pick on them, because we all have the same problem: On the primal level of appetite, the idea that tasty, convenient, low-cost foods may someday kill us just does not compute. We see something that looks good and want to eat it now, deeply discounting what may happen 30 to 40 years down the road. Choosing healthy foods instead, and finding the balance between what we eat and what we work off in our daily lives, is by contrast a highly abstract calculation that requires long-term willpower.

Wansink talks about the diet "you don't know you're on." He's the man who does studies on how we decide when to eat (or stop eating), like his famous one with soup bowls that were imperceptibly refilled through a hidden tube (folks ate more from them). Wansink has examined dozens of cues that can lead us to eat too much.

Taking Steps to Address the Problem

The key question about obesity, he says, is "What can reasonably be done by a person tonight? You're not going to change capitalism. You're not going to eliminate food companies and go back to the days of picking berries. So what can you do tonight?" We can eat 200 to 300 calories more or less from one day to the next without noticing, Wansink says. That's how we grow huge in the first place. But using little tricks to work this "mindless margin" is also a way to become thin.

Wansink's studies all led to his basic rule that large packages and containers unleash large appetites: bowls of snacks, beakers of booze, dessert platters—any container. Even advocates of moderation like bartenders and physicians tended to supersize in his studies. "The answer is to use a smaller container," he says. It also helps to separate yourself from food.

179

Move cookies from eye level to the back of the cabinet. Break up the jumbo box of food into smaller portions. Leave serving bowls on the kitchen counter instead of the table. "It makes people think twice about whether they want to have that second, third, or fourth helping," he says.

Many casual-dining chains have switched from short, wide glasses to tall, thin ones to avoid the overpouring effect. Some companies have found profit in the 100-calorie snack pack. And companies are increasingly reducing sugar or salt without trumpeting it on the package, he says, and customers rarely notice. Today's Golden Crisp cereal might taste different from the Super Sugar Crisp we ate years ago. "But we don't have side-by-side comparisons, so we don't say, 'Wait a minute, it's not as mind-numbingly brain-rushful as it was 12 years ago.'"

More Steps Are Needed

Given the scale of the crisis, though, are any of these efforts enough? Childhood obesity now affects 17 percent of the school-age population in the United States, up from 5 percent before 1980. One child in three is overweight. To some experts, like psychologist Kelly Brownell, Ph.D., director of Yale University's Rudd Center for Food Policy and Obesity, small plates and voluntary reforms by food companies won't cut it.

Brownell argues that the best way to change our obesogenic environment is by taking on the big drivers of obesity in the food industry, and by that he means using fat taxes and regulatory reforms. There is precedent for this large-scale action, he says, in the face of such a threat to public health—compulsory vaccinations for schoolchildren, community fluoridation of water to fight tooth decay, and the decades-long battle against tobacco. "Children were being harmed, and society felt justified stepping in," he says. It's the same now, he argues, with obesity.

Sweetness and fat are the two dietary delights we crave most, and food manufacturers are ingenious at finding new ways to deliver them to us. They approach the marketplace—your belly and mine—with what can seem to critics like a feedlot mentality. It's not that they intend to make us fat. They advertise only to increase market share, they say.

Sweetness and fat are the two dietary delights we crave most, and food manufacturers are ingenious at finding new ways to deliver them to us.

Sweet Tooth

Let's start with sweetness: Sugar was a costly luxury until the 18th century, when mills in Brazil and the West Indies ramped up production, lowering prices and boosting consumption. "The glories of the Renaissance were created on the basis of a teaspoonful per head of sugar per year," Henry Hobhouse wrote in his agricultural history *Seeds of Change*. The average American consumes *45 pounds of sugar a year*—that's 4,900 teaspoons, and no Renaissance in sight.

We also consume 36 pounds annually of a sweetener that wasn't even an option until the 1970s—high-fructose corn syrup, otherwise known as HFCS. For about $1.50, a single 64-ounce Double Gulp soda from 7-Eleven can provide what was once a lifetime dose of sweetener.

But food is cheap and abundant. The food supply in the United States now bulges with an estimated 3,800 calories a day per person, almost twice what we need. So profits often come from getting people to eat more food or food that's more energy-dense—packed with more sweetness, fat, or some unholy union of the two. The handful of corporations that dominate the food market drive up our appetites with relentless advertising, outlets on every corner, bigger portions, and price tinkering to make larger orders seem more appealing, according to a 2004 paper coauthored by Mickey Chopra, M.D., Ph.D., now UNICEF's [the United Nations Children's Fund's] chief of health.

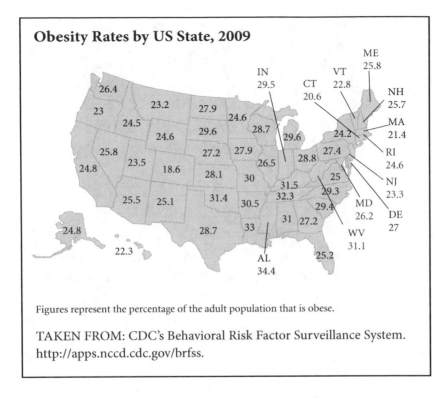

Obesity Rates by US State, 2009

Figures represent the percentage of the adult population that is obese.

TAKEN FROM: CDC's Behavioral Risk Factor Surveillance System. http://apps.nccd.cdc.gov/brfss.

The Lure of New Products

New products add to the problem. Manufacturers used to introduce about 250 new candy and snack products a year in the United States, Greg Critser reports in his 2003 book *Fat Land: How Americans Became the Fattest People in the World.* By the late 1980s, that number had jumped to 2,000, fueled in part by the entry of HFCS into the food supply. This corn-based sweetener, which is cheaper to make than cane sugar, has chemical properties that food companies love. It protects frozen foods against freezer burn. It keeps long-shelf-life items—like those in vending machines—fresh tasting. "Using it in bakery products (even in rolls and biscuits that normally contained no sugar) made them look more 'natural'—as if they'd just been browned in the oven," Critser wrote. With the surge of new products, snacking boomed, particularly among people under 40. They now take in more than a quarter of their calories from snacks.

Some research has questioned whether HFCS, the accidental elixir of our feedlot, may disrupt hormones that control appetite and induce people to eat more. HFCS now accounts for 42 percent of the sweeteners in our food and almost all the sweeteners in our non-diet soft drinks.

The average American drinks about 16 ounces of soda a day, up about 33 percent since 1980—and 500 percent from 1950 to 1999. Incredibly, that makes soft drinks the number one food consumed in the American diet, according to the health economist Eric A. Finkelstein, Ph.D., and Laurie Zuckerman, coauthors of *The Fattening of America*.

"If the average American drank water instead of sugar-sweetened beverages," they wrote, "he would weigh about 15 pounds less than he does now." If tap water seems too plain, brew tea. Convincing the nation to cut back on soft drinks wouldn't end the obesity epidemic. But it would make a good start.

The Case for a Soda Tax

Brownell says a soda tax is a necessary weapon in the war against obesity. About 30 states already tax soda in some form, mostly at rates somewhat higher than other taxed food items. But a RAND Corporation study this year estimated that it would take an 18 percent tax—not the current average of 4 percent—to produce a significant drop in soda consumption. By comparison, taxes on cigarettes account for up to 61 percent of the cost of a pack and have proved highly effective at reducing tobacco use. The beverage industry argues that soda in moderation is not harmful and that such taxes would mainly hurt poor people.

But to Brownell, what's happening now with soda is "precisely what happened" in the debate over tobacco. The evidence connecting sugared drinks to obesity, diabetes, and heart disease is "rock solid," he says, and these drinks are "aggressively marketed, especially to children."

Brownell says beverage companies employ the same kind of strategies that tobacco lobbyists once employed. That includes reliance on so-called citizens' groups that are actually fronts for the industry, he says. Among them are Americans Against Food Taxes and New Yorkers Against Unfair Taxes. One prominent group, the Center for Consumer Freedom, actually had its start as a tobacco industry front but is now waging the fight against what it calls "an epidemic of obesity myths."

Marketing Junk Food to Children

Beyond soda taxes, the obesogenic-environment camp argues that an important way to fight obesity is to limit the marketing of unhealthy products to children. The beverage industry says it's already doing that voluntarily. Earlier this year it touted a study that found that TV advertising of sweetened drinks to children and teens had dropped by as much as 30 percent over a 4-year period.

But the same study found that advertising targeted at children by fast-food companies was up as much as 20 percent. And a 2007 Kaiser [Family] Foundation study found that children typically view 30 to 50 hours of food advertising a year, mostly ads promoting candy, snacks, sweetened cereals, or fast food—and none for fruits or vegetables.

Beyond soda taxes, the obesogenic-environment camp argues that an important way to fight obesity is to limit the marketing of unhealthy products to children.

The industry's fallback response? Exercise. Americans are too sedentary and spend too much time in front of the television. The obesity problem wouldn't exist if we all exercised, the CEO of PepsiCo said in a *Fortune* interview this year. And it's hard to argue with the message that exercise is good. In other words, the problem isn't the food industry; *it's you*. And there's nothing wrong with our feedlot. You just need to add an exercise wheel.

"There's a tremendous seduction in pointing the finger at somebody else," says Wansink. "If parents can blame the school system for their overweight child, or blame food commercials, or blame fast-food or candy companies, they don't have to say, 'Hey, maybe I'm the one who's messing up, having cookies all over the kitchen counter and letting him eat pizza while he watches TV.' Being able to point at somebody else means we can just go back to doing what we want—which is come home from work and not have to do anything."

The Model of Somerville

But there is a middle ground, and I found it in Somerville, Massachusetts. This American city of 76,000 people is trying to do something about its typically severe obesity problem. I made an appointment with Nicole Rioles, coordinator of the Shape Up Somerville program, whose idea of a media tour means hopping on bikes and riding the city's seven hills and 4 square miles.

City transportation planner Kathleen Ziegenfuss joined us, also on a bike. "It's really quick and you don't have to deal with parking," she said. She outlined a plan to add 10 miles of bike paths and "sharrows" (arrows indicating that bikes and cars have equal rights to the road) this year, and she also described a longer-term plan to extend a community footpath and bike path another 2 1/2 miles through the city, at a cost of $20 million to $30 million.

She mapped out sidewalks that will be widened for pedestrian traffic, and described a program that would shut down some roads to vehicles for community events. (Like dozens of such programs worldwide, it was inspired by the 30-year-old

Ciclovía program in Bogotá, Colombia.) The city is also working on mass-transit improvements that will put every neighborhood in Somerville within an easy walk to a train or bus.

It was 8 a.m., and kids and parents were taking to the
sidewalks in loose packs—"walking school buses," an idea borrowed from Lecco, Italy—to reach class safely and on foot. We
pedaled off to a park, one of a dozen the city has added or
renovated. For a mid-morning snack, we stopped at Amigos
Market, which earned a "Shape Up Somerville" sticker for selling packs of sliced pineapple and mango for a buck. For lunch,
it was the Neighborhood Restaurant and Bakery, which puts
out the huge portions customers like but now displays table
cards suggesting that they take half of it home or ask to have
it cooked in canola oil instead of butter.

In the city's school system, the food-service director re-
called the student boycott when she removed the deep fryer
from the high school. (Then kids got used to eating healthier
stuff, and lunch program participation increased.) Grade-
schoolers also eat their vegetables, she said, when she cooks
them well and markets them with names like X-Ray Vision
carrots—borrowing from Wansink's research showing that our
eating habits are unduly influenced by catchy labels.

Providing a Healthier Environment

Later, Rioles and I pedaled to City Hall to visit Mayor Joseph
Curtatone, who has not personally accepted the bicycle as his
savior. But he hits the gym at 5 a.m. and, at the age of 44,
runs a 4:30 marathon. Curtatone wants to change land-use
rules that force people to hop into cars and drive to mega
food stores in the suburbs. He wants to bring back neighborhood produce stands. He wants to take major thoroughfares
that were turned into high-speed commuter "on-off ramps" to
nearby downtown Boston, and recapture them for the people
of Somerville. He thinks the streets should be safe enough to
let "free-range kids" run out the door to play.

"Our goal is not to tell you what to eat," he says. "Our goal is not to tell you how to act. Our goal is to develop systems that give you the best choices, and make those choices easier for you." Despite the vast scale of the change, he says, the important thing is to make sure "every step you take, all your strategic attacks, are aligned to this overall goal," which he likes to sum up in a phrase: "Eat smart, play hard."

On the way out the door, we bump into George Landers, the superintendent of buildings and grounds, a department traditionally staffed by big-bellied men in thrall to internal combustion engines. Not an easy sell, I figured. But Landers says he and his wife walk an hour every morning, not counting the walk to work, and eat healthier food. At 60, he's dropped 40 pounds, trimmed his belt size from 46 to 40, and cut his diabetes meds and blood-sugar level by half and his blood pressure by a third. "I have more energy now than I've had in years," he adds. "My doctor says I'm a miracle."

Can that miracle work for our entire big-bellied country? "It takes decades to make a change," Rioles warns. "If we can influence 100 small changes in the course of the day," she says, "we can help people make healthier choices." And if those changes add up, maybe we will lose weight the way we got fat, almost without noticing it.

France Takes Proactive Measures to Fight Obesity

Mildrade Cherfils

Mildrade Cherfils is a contributor to GlobalPost, an online international news agency. In the following viewpoint, she surveys the measures that France is taking to combat its growing obesity problem. Cherfils reports that a 2009 panel of French health experts recommended a nationwide physical fitness and nutrition program in French schools to help fight childhood obesity, and it has allocated funds for a nationwide plan to combat obesity.

As you read, consider the following questions:

1. How many French students will participate in a voluntary program about exercise and nutrition called "Morning Classes, Afternoon Sports"?
2. What percentage of French adults are considered obese, as noted by the author?
3. According to the viewpoint, how much is America's diet industry worth?

It's almost an unthinkable admission: the French concerned about their weight?

Yet when the French school year begins this fall [2010], more than 7,000 students will find themselves the volunteers in an experiment to improve awareness about health and

Mildrade Cherfils, "French Schools on Front Line of Obesity Fight," GlobalPost, September 8, 2010. Reproduced by permission.

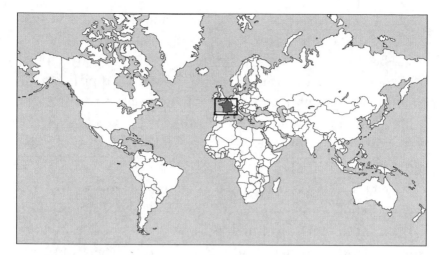

physical fitness—and which coincides with official concerns about rising obesity rates in France.

The project, baptized "Morning Classes, Afternoon Sports," and taking effect in 124 middle and high schools across the country and in overseas departments, was devised as an antidote to school violence and absenteeism and as a way to help students develop team-building skills, according to Luc Chatel, the French education minister.

But the program's other inevitable benefits are consistent with recommendations by a panel of health experts commissioned in 2009 by President Nicolas Sarkozy to devise a plan for addressing rising obesity in France.

More physical activity at school—whether as a result of installing basketball courts or game posts in school yards—promotes physical activity as a way of life, according to one of the 19 suggestions intended to help France stay ahead of the prevention curve.

The Scope of the Crisis

Not that the average French person needs to give up buttery pastries, rich sauces and red wine tomorrow.

"The so-called obesity epidemic is about 20 years behind the United States and 10 years behind Great Britain," said Arnaud Basdevant, a nutritionist and expert on obesity tapped by Élysée to lead the team that will ultimately implement the country's three-year action plan to fight obesity that came out of the commission's findings. "This time lag shows that France was committed to the prevention and management of obesity somewhat earlier than the U.S. and the U.K."

Roughly 14.5 percent of the adult population—about 6.5 million people—was considered obese in 2009 compared with 8.5 percent in 1997, according to figures from the latest ObEpi Roche survey, which has been monitoring the nation's expanding waistline since 1997. Every three years, the national institute of health and medical research, Inserm, and market research company TNS Sofres distribute 20,000 questionnaires to households in order to study the evolution of obesity.

Despite the progressive increase, France's obesity levels are close to those of the United States in the late 1970s, said Basdevant and Susan Yager, a New York City–based writer and lecturer on nutrition and food. But an average of 250,000 people joining those ranks every year is helping to close that gap, whether the reason is the creep of fast food into the French diet, people working outside the home having less time for long meals or evolving values.

A Proactive Approach

The country's early adoption of a proactive approach is credited with some successes. Since 2001, Basdevant said, France has had an established National Health and Nutrition Program, a Ministry of Health initiative that has included obesity prevention.

In 2004, when health officials found that the percentage of overweight young people had climbed to 17 percent in 20 years, the government responded by removing all soda and snack machines from the 20 percent of middle schools and 50 percent of high schools that carried them.

The national health program is credited with stabilizing weight gain and obesity in children, improving the amount of fruit and vegetables consumed by adults and helping to reduce the population's salt intake, according to a national health survey conducted in 2006 and presented in 2007 by the French Institute for Public Health Surveillance, a public institution that reports to the Ministry of Health.

There are plans to go further. Following the presidential panel's report issued in December, Sarkozy announced in a letter addressed to Basdevant in June that he was setting aside 140 million euros to implement a national obesity plan over the next three years.

[France's] early adoption of a proactive approach is credited with some successes.

The Plan

The plan is three-pronged, Basdevant said. The first component aims to create centers for medical care and surgical treatment of obesity and to organize a "care chain." A research component, as a second element, will look at various factors that contribute to obesity, including economic and social dimensions while prevention, as a third component, will be established gradually.

"It is a multi-factorial disease resulting from the interaction of biological, behavioral, environmental and economic factors," Basdevant explained in an email message. "The preventive strategy is therefore highly complex and can only be multi-focal and multi-partner."

The national approach contrasts with that of weight-loss programs like Jenny Craig, as it "pushes ahead with a successful solution to address a major public health issue," according

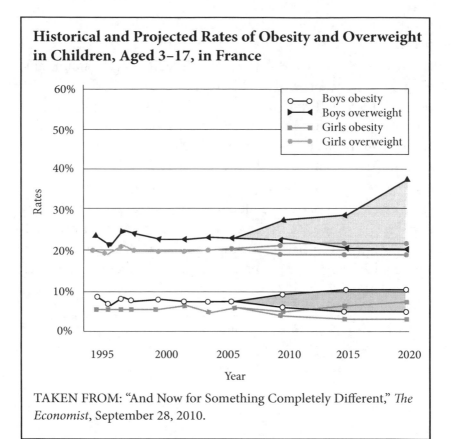

Historical and Projected Rates of Obesity and Overweight in Children, Aged 3–17, in France

Legend:
- ○—○ Boys obesity
- ►—◄ Boys overweight
- ■—■ Girls obesity
- ●—● Girls overweight

TAKEN FROM: "And Now for Something Completely Different," *The Economist*, September 28, 2010.

to a press release issued by Nestlé in March when the program that "combines its ready-made meals with individual consultation" arrived on the French market. Jenny Craig offers a personalized program that requires customers seeking to lose weight to eat prepackaged meals available for purchase at the company's weight loss centers.

Valerie Berrebi, a spokeswoman for Nestlé who handles the Jenny Craig account, said colleagues with direct knowledge of how the program was faring in France so far were unavailable for comment since most were just returning from summer holiday.

"They were indeed a solution looking for a problem," Yager said, referring to Jenny Craig. Her latest book, *The Hun-*

dred Year Diet, focuses on America's $55 billion diet industry and the "national obsession with food, dieting, deprivation, and weight loss."

French Attitudes Toward Food

The French attitude toward food, she noted, is very different, as France has always put such a premium on nutrition. To illustrate just how much, Yager, who is based in New York but said she travels to France at least once a year, cited examples of French children being weighed at schools and letters sent home to parents to alert them about any weight-related problems. In the United States, she said, such intervention might yield a reaction from parents of "don't tell us what to feed our children."

"They have got to resist the impulse to give in to the quick and easy fixes," said Yager, who said she would be disappointed to see France go down the diet route. "That is going to catch up with people."

The French attitude toward food . . . is very different, as France has always put such a premium on nutrition.

Closing the nutritional divide is one of the areas Basdevant and his colleagues will focus on in implementing a national plan. They'll also be looking more closely at economic factors, since obesity has greater impact on the lower socioeconomic segment of society, according to research cited by Basdevant and Jean-Michel Oppert, both of whom worked with the government commission.

"It's not about finding a scapegoat and believing that in beating that we've solved the problem," Basdevant said. He advocates acting on a variety of axes, ranging from the environment to a city's transport policy, from the meals served to children at school to individual behavior.

"It is a lengthy process," he said, "but any preventive action requires time."

Japan Outlaws Obesity

Norimitsu Onishi

Norimitsu Onishi is a Canadian journalist. In the following viewpoint, he reports on the latest efforts of Japanese officials to curb obesity—a fat law, also known as "metabo" law, which regulates the waistline size of adult women and men. Onishi maintains that despite criticisms that the limits are too stringent, the government hopes that the metabo law will shrink the number of overweight and obese people in Japan, thereby saving the government money in health care costs, one of the country's most serious financial problems.

As you read, consider the following questions:

1. As outlined in the viewpoint, what percentage of the Japanese population will be measured every year?
2. How much does the Japanese government aim to shrink the overweight population between 2008–2012, according to the viewpoint?
3. According to the viewpoint, why has the word "metabo" made it easier for health care providers to urge their patients to lose weight?

In the land of the Sumo wrestler, where the prowess of sportsmen is regularly judged by their massive girth, one of the world's most ambitious anti-obesity campaigns is under way.

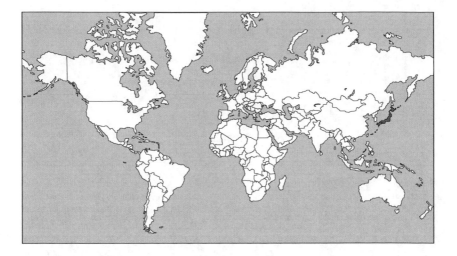

Summoned by the city of Amagasaki one recent morning, Minoru Nogiri, 45, a flower shop owner, found himself lining up to have his waistline measured. With no visible paunch, he seemed to run little risk of being classified as overweight, or metabo, the preferred word in Japan these days.

But because the new limit for male waistlines was a strict 33.5 inches, he had anxiously measured himself at home a couple of days earlier. "I'm on the borderline," he said.

The Metabo Law

Under a national law that came into effect two months ago [April 2008], companies and local governments must measure the waistlines of Japanese people between the ages of 40 and 74 as part of their annual checkups. That represents more than 56 million waistlines, or about 44% of the entire population.

Those exceeding government limits and suffering from a weight-related ailment will be given dieting guidance if, after three months, they do not lose weight. If necessary, those people will be steered towards further re-education after six more months.

The limits of 33.5 inches for men and 35.4 inches for women are identical to thresholds established in 2005 for Japan by the International Diabetes Federation as an easy guideline for identifying health risks.

To reach its goals of shrinking the overweight population by 10% over the next four years and 25% over the next seven years, the government will impose financial penalties on companies and local governments that fail to meet specific targets. The country's Ministry of Health[, Labour and Welfare] argues that the campaign will keep the spread of diseases like diabetes and strokes in check.

The [Japanese health] ministry says that curbing widening waistlines will rein in a rapidly ageing society's ballooning health care costs, one of the most serious and politically delicate problems facing Japan today.

Decreasing Costs

The ministry also says that curbing widening waistlines will rein in a rapidly ageing society's ballooning health care costs, one of the most serious and politically delicate problems facing Japan today. Most Japanese are covered under public health care or through their work. Anger over a plan that would make those aged 75 and older pay more for health care recently brought a parliamentary censure motion against Prime Minister Yasuo Fukuda, the first against a prime minister in the country's post-war history.

But critics say that the government guidelines are simply too strict, and that more than half of all men will be considered overweight. The effect, they say, will be to encourage overmedication and ultimately raise health care costs.

In Amagasaki, a city in western Japan, officials have moved aggressively to measure waistlines in what the government calls special checkups. They aimed to measure at least 65% of

---

Is the Metabo Law a Good Idea?

The Japanese plan to deal with metabo is innovative and does express the nation's recognition of the [obesity problem]. However, it's not the right approach for Japan or any other country. No politician in the US would escape impeachment if he/she proposed such a thing, which could only happen after a long night of boozing with pharmaceutical industry lobbyists.

Donald Ardell, "A Japanese Plan to Help Employees Lose Weight," Ezinearticles.com, January 25, 2011. http://ezinearticles.com.

---

the 40- to 74-year-olds covered by public health insurance, an "extremely difficult" goal, acknowledged Midori Noguchi, a city official.

When his turn came, Nogiri, the flower shop owner, entered a booth where he bared his midriff, exposing a flat stomach with barely discernible love handles. A nurse wrapped a tape measure around his waist across his belly button: 33.6 inches, or 0.1 inch over the limit.

"Strikeout," he said, defeat spreading across his face.

The Origins of the Metabo Law

The campaign started a couple of years ago when the health ministry began beating the drums for a medical condition that few Japanese had ever heard of—metabolic syndrome—a collection of factors that heighten the risk of developing vascular disease and diabetes. Those include abdominal obesity, high blood pressure and high levels of blood glucose and cholesterol. In no time, the condition was popularly shortened to the funny-sounding metabo, and it has become the nation's shorthand for obesity.

The mayor of one town in Mie, a region near Amagasaki, became so wrapped up in the anti-metabo campaign that he and six other town officials formed a weight-loss group called "The Seven Metabo Samurai." That campaign ended abruptly after a 47-year-old member with a 39-inch waistline died of a heart attack while jogging.

Still, at a city gym in Amagasaki recently, dozens of residents—few of whom appeared overweight—danced to the city's anti-metabo song, which warned against trouser buttons popping and flying away, "pyun-pyun-pyun!"

"Goodbye, metabolic. Let's get our checkups together. Go! Go! Go! Goodbye, metabolic. Don't wait till you get sick. No! No! No!"

The word metabo has made it easier for health care providers to urge their patients to lose weight, said Dr Yoshikuni Sakamoto, a physician in the employee health insurance union at Matsushita, which makes Panasonic products. "Before, we had to broach the issue with the word obesity, which definitely has a negative image," he said. "But metabo sounds much more inclusive."

The Law and Corporations

Even before Tokyo's directives, Matsushita had focused on its employees' weight during their annual checkups. Last summer, Akio Inoue, 30, an engineer carrying 17 stone on a 5ft 7in frame, was told by a company physician to lose weight or take medication for his high blood pressure. After dieting, he was down to 182 pounds, but his waistline was still more than one inch over the state-approved limit.

With the new law, Matsushita has to measure the waistlines of not only its employees but also their families and pensioners. As part of its intensifying efforts, the company has started giving its employees "metabo check" towels that double as tape measures.

Companies like Matsushita must measure the waistlines of at least 80% of their employees and get 10% of those deemed metabolic to lose weight by 2012.

NEC, Japan's largest maker of PCs [personal computers], said that if it failed to meet its targets, it could incur £9.7m in penalties.

Periodical and Internet Sources Bibliography

The following articles have been selected to supplement the diverse views presented in this chapter.

Zosia Bielski	"Can Obese People Be Bribed to Walk?" *Globe & Mail*, November 30, 2010.
Pascale Bonnefoy	"Combating Chile's Exploding Obesity Rates," GlobalPost, June 4, 2010. www.globalpost.com.
Maria Cheng	"Stomach Pacemaker Could Help Obese Lose Weight," Associated Press, March 3, 2011.
Kate Dailey	"Can Laws Fix the Obesity Crisis?" *Newsweek*, November 16, 2010.
Aaron Derfel	"The War Against Obesity," *Montreal Gazette*, March 25, 2011.
Daniel Engber	"Let Them Drink Water!" Slate.com, September 21, 2009. www.slate.com.
Christy Harrison	"Slimming the Future," Slate.com, February 18, 2011. www.slate.com.
David Haslam	"Commentary: Banning Trans Fats Is a Start," *Telegraph*, October 15, 2007.
David Katz	"Why Holistic Nutrition Is the Best Approach," *Huffington Post*, April 1, 2011. www.huffington post.com.
Meredith Melnick	"Weight-Loss Winner: Gastric Bypass Works Better for Obese Patients," *Time*, February 22, 2011.
Wang Wei	"Beijing Fights Obesity with Tape Measures," *China Post*, January 23, 2010.

For Further Discussion

Chapter 1

1. In his viewpoint, Ross Gittins contends that most developed nations have a major obesity crisis. The *Age*, however, reveals that experts believe that the reporting of the childhood obesity problem has been overblown. After reading both viewpoints, which view do you feel is presented more persuasively and why?

2. This chapter examines countries and regions that are experiencing an obesity epidemic. Which country most surprised you? Cite specific statistics or examples from that country.

Chapter 2

1. How do cultural factors influence body image in society? Read the viewpoint originally published in the *Kuwait Times* that explores how Mauritanian women are pressured to be obese. How does this differ from where you live? What pressures do young men and women face when it comes to weight?

2. Several of the viewpoints in this chapter discuss how economic factors influence obesity. Read the viewpoints by George F. Will and Nina Martyris to determine how obesity affects the social and economic classes in America and India. Why are the two countries mirror images of each other? How can each country address its own obesity epidemic?

Chapter 3

1. This chapter touches on several of the effects of the obesity crisis. Read every viewpoint and identify which effect

you feel is the most dangerous. How can governments address the dangerous results of growing rates of obesity?

Chapter 4

1. In his viewpoint, Richard Reeves discusses the need to create government policies to address obesity that respect individual freedom. In your opinion, how far should governments go to address problems like obesity that are considered a public health issue? Use Reeves's viewpoint to inform your answer.

2. Which of the policies reviewed in this chapter appeal to you as an effective way to address obesity in your community? Which one seems ineffective or unworkable?

Organizations to Contact

The editors have compiled the following list of organizations concerned with the issues debated in this book. The descriptions are derived from materials provided by the organizations. All have publications or information available for interested readers. The list was compiled on the date of publication of the present volume; the information provided here may change. Be aware that many organizations take several weeks or longer to respond to inquiries, so allow as much time as possible.

American Medical Association (AMA)

515 N. State Street, Chicago, IL   60654
(800) 621-8335
website: www.ama-assn.org

The American Medical Association (AMA) was established in 1847 to improve the state of the American health system and the health of Americans. In the fight against obesity, the AMA brings health professionals together to formulate more effective strategies to treat overweight and obese patients and facilitate weight loss. The association works to allocate resources, research, and treatment for the growing epidemic of obesity and provides fact sheets and studies for health care professionals who deal with the problem and weight-related disease. The AMA publishes *JAMA: The Journal of the American Medical Association*, a world-renowned periodical that researches health issues and treatments, and the *AMA Wire*, a weekly e-newsletter that features breaking medical news and information on topics of interest. The AMA website offers access to a wide range of resources, including other e-newsletters and journals that cover more specific topics.

American Society for Nutrition (ASN)

9650 Rockville Pike, Bethesda, MD   20814
(301) 634-7050 • fax: (301) 634-7892
website: www.nutrition.org

The American Society for Nutrition (ASN) is a nonprofit organization devoted to nutrition research and applying the latest knowledge about nutrition and weight management to help humans and animals. The ASN works to bring clinical nutritionists and other health care professionals together to advance the latest developments in the nutrition and weight management field and provide training to those working in the industry. The ASN publishes the *American Journal of Clinical Nutrition*, a monthly journal available on the organization's website. Also available online are the *Journal of Nutrition, Advances in Nutrition*, and several e-newsletters, podcasts, and blogs.

Australian and New Zealand Obesity Society
Medical Foundation Building K2
University of Sydney   NSW 2006
   Australia
e-mail: office@asso.org.au
website: www.asso.org.au

The Australian and New Zealand Obesity Society is a membership organization of health care professionals—doctors, nurse practitioners, dieticians, nutritionists, and scientists—focused on the growing problem of obesity in Australia, New Zealand, and the Pacific region. The association was formed in order to disseminate the latest research on and treatment of obesity, as well as the health problems that are a direct result of obesity, including diabetes, heart disease, and hypertension. Members meet up in various forums to exchange ideas and information and train in the latest techniques and treatments. The society's website offers updates on the latest events and health initiatives in the region, as well as links to other organizations and obesity-related journals.

Canadian Obesity Network (CON)
Royal Alexandra Hospital, Room 102
Materials Management Centre
10240 Kingsway Avenue, Edmonton   AB T5H 3V9

(780) 735-6764 • fax: (780) 735-6763
e-mail: info@obesitynetwork.ca
website: www.obesitynetwork.ca

The Canadian Obesity Network (CON) is a nonprofit organization that coordinates obesity funding, research, prevention, and treatment. The group is focused on three key goals— addressing the social stigma associated with obesity; improving the way health care professionals work with patients with obesity; and providing access to weight management and weight loss programs. CON has launched the Online Best Evidence Service in Tackling Obesity Plus (OBESITY+), which offers the most recent information and tools to help health care providers in all aspects of obesity management and treatment. The CON website features a range of research, presentations, and other resources for members and nonmembers.

European Association for the Study of Obesity (EASO)

113–119 High Street, Hampton Hill, Middlesex   TW12 1NJ
  United Kingdom
(+44) (0) 20 8783 2256 • fax: (+44) (0) 20 8979 6700
e-mail: enquiries@easo.org
website: www.easoobesity.org

The European Association for the Study of Obesity (EASO) is a membership organization that works to "promote research into obesity, facilitate contact between individuals and organisations, and promote action that tackles the epidemic of obesity" in the countries of the European Union. Through programs like HOPE: Health Promotion Through Obesity Prevention Across Europe, EASO lobbies for and supports effective and wide-ranging weight reduction policies and aims to bring the problem of obesity to the forefront of public awareness in Europe. EASO publishes *Obesity Facts*, a journal that explores cutting-edge research on obesity and weight-related disease, as well as new developments and initiatives in the field.

Food and Agriculture Organization of the United Nations (FAO)

Viale delle Terme di Caracalla, Rome   00153
   Italy
(+39) 06 57051 • fax: (+39) 06 570 53152
e-mail: FAO-HQ@fao.org
website: www.fao.org

The Food and Agriculture Organization (FAO) is a United Nations agency tasked with leading the global fight against hunger. FAO marshals international cooperation to forge agreements and policies that work to provide food to those who need it and develop agricultural policies that benefit citizens and wildlife. Although its main focus is alleviating hunger, FAO is also addressing the growing epidemic of global obesity. The agency has compiled and published a range of research and policy briefs on overweight and obesity, particularly the trend of countries with high rates of both malnutrition and obesity. FAO publishes a number of reports including "The State of Food and Agriculture" and "The State of Food Insecurity in the World."

International Association for the Study of Obesity (IASO)

Charles Darwin House, 12 Roger Street, London   WCIN 2JU
   United Kingdom
(+44) 20 7685 2580 • fax: (+44) 20 7685 2581
e-mail: enquiries@iaso.org
website: www.iaso.org

The International Association for the Study of Obesity (IASO) is a nonprofit, international organization that brings together forty-two national organizations specializing in the study of obesity. According to the IASO mission statement, the group strives to "improve global health by promoting the understanding of obesity and weight-related diseases through scientific research and dialogue, whilst encouraging the development of effective policies for their prevention and management." To that end, IASO provides access to the latest research on the management and prevention of obesity, as well as summaries of new anti-obesity programs and policies. This information can be found in IASO's publications, which include the *International Journal of Obesity, Clinical Obesity*, and *Obesity Reviews*.

National Obesity Forum (NOF)

First Floor, 6a Gordon Road, Nottingham   NG2 5LN
   United Kingdom
(+44) 0115 846 2109 • fax: (+44) 0115 846 2329
e-mail: info@nof.uk.com
website: www.nationalobesityforum.org.uk

The National Obesity Forum (NOF) is a membership organization in the United Kingdom that brings together health care professionals in order to raise awareness of the obesity epidemic and the deleterious health effects of overweight and obesity on the individual and the National Health Service. The NOF aims to make weight management a higher priority in health treatment and to sharpen the focus on weight loss to prevent weight-related diseases that are growing in Britain, Scotland, Wales, and Northern Ireland. NOF sponsors conferences, lectures, and forums to help spread the message about the obesity epidemic and weight management programs.

Obesity Society

8757 Georgia Avenue, Ste. 1320, Silver Spring, MD   20910
(301) 563-6526 • fax: (301) 563-6595
website: www.obesity.org

The Obesity Society is devoted to addressing the growing global obesity epidemic. It funds and disseminates research on overweight and obesity; promotes policies that address issues related to obesity and obesity-related diseases; offers a forum for scientists and health care professionals to exchange information on obesity; and develops and lobbies for effective weight management programs and health initiatives aiming to improve individual and community health. The Obesity Society sponsors an annual scientific meeting, the largest conference in North America focusing on obesity research, treatment, and prevention. The society also publishes *Obesity*, a journal that offers the latest research and commentary in the field.

Royal Society of Medicine

1 Wimpole Street, London   W1G 0AE
   United Kingdom
(+44) (0) 20 7290 2900 • fax: (+44) (0) 20 7290 2989
website: www.rsm.ac.uk

The Royal Society of Medicine is the largest provider of medical education in the United Kingdom. The independent association has developed a range of educational programs and activities meant to keep health care professionals updated on the latest research, treatment programs, and medical information available. It also offers a forum for doctors, nurses, dentists, and other health professionals to exchange ideas and techniques. The Royal Society of Medicine publishes the *Journal of the Royal Society of Medicine*, a monthly periodical that covers the latest research and in-depth articles on medical topics, including weight management treatments.

World Health Organization (WHO)

Avenue Appia 20, Geneva 27   1211
   Switzerland
(+41) 22 791 21 11 • fax: (+41) 22 791 31 11
e-mail: info@who.int
website: www.who.int

The World Health Organization (WHO) is the United Nations agency responsible for directing global health care matters. WHO funds research into health issues that affect global health, including the obesity epidemic and weight-related diseases. The agency monitors health trends, compiles useful statistics, and offers technical support to countries dealing with the consequences of growing rates of obesity. WHO's website features podcasts, blogs, and videos; it also offers fact sheets, reports, studies, and a calendar of events. There are a broad range of articles on nutrition-related topics on the website.

Bibliography of Books

Zoltan J. Acs and Alan Lyles, eds. *Obesity, Business, and Public Policy.* Cheltenham, UK: Edward Elgar, 2007.

Elliot M. Blass, ed. *Obesity: Causes, Mechanisms, Prevention, and Treatment.* Sunderland, MA: Sinauer Associates, 2008.

George A. Bray *The Metabolic Syndrome and Obesity.* Totowa, NJ: Humana Press, 2007.

Eric A. Finkelstein and Laurie Zuckerman *The Fattening of America: How the Economy Makes Us Fat, if It Matters, and What to Do About It.* Hoboken, NJ: Wiley, 2008.

Richard K. Flamenbaum, ed. *Global Dimensions of Childhood Obesity.* New York: Nova Science Publishers, 2007.

Michael Gard *The End of the Obesity Epidemic.* London: Routledge, 2011.

Stephen Kline *Globesity, Food Marketing, and Family Lifestyles.* New York: Palgrave Macmillan, 2011.

Peter G. Kopelman, Ian D. Caterson, and William H. Dietz, eds. *Clinical Obesity in Adults and Children.* 3rd ed. Hoboken, NJ: Wiley-Blackwell, 2010.

Mario Mazzocchi, W. Bruce Traill, and Jason F. Shogren *Fat Economics: Nutrition, Health, and Economic Policy.* New York: Oxford University Press, 2009.

Heather McLannahan and Pete Clifton, eds.

Challenging Obesity: The Science Behind the Issues. New York: Oxford University Press, 2008.

Stacy Ann Mitchell and Teri D. Mitchell

Livin' Large: African-American Sisters Confront Obesity. Munster, IN: Hilton Publishing Co., 2008.

Wendy Murphy

Weight and Health. Minneapolis, MN: Twenty-First Century Books, 2008.

Derek J. Oddy, Peter J. Atkins, and Virginie Amilien

The Rise of Obesity in Europe: A Twentieth Century Food History. Burlington, VT: Ashgate, 2009.

Barry Popkin

The World Is Fat: The Fads, Trends, Policies, and Products That Are Fattening the Human Race. New York: Avery, 2009.

Michael L. Power and Jay Schulkin

The Evolution of Obesity. Baltimore, MD: Johns Hopkins University Press, 2009.

Emma Rich, Lee F. Monaghan, and Lucy Aphramor, eds.

Debating Obesity: Critical Perspectives. New York: Palgrave Macmillan, 2010.

Jennifer T. Rogers, ed.

Gastric Bypass: Surgical Procedures, Health Effects and Common Complications. New York: Nova Science Publishers, 2010.

Barry Sears

Toxic Fat: When Good Fat Turns Bad. Nashville, TN: Thomas Nelson, 2008.

Carol M. Segel, ed. — *Childhood Obesity: Risk Factors, Health Effects, and Prevention.* Hauppauge, NY: Nova Science Publishers, 2010.

Kerry Segrave — *Obesity in America, 1850–1939: A History of Social Attitudes and Treatment.* Jefferson, NC: McFarland & Co., 2008.

Wolfgang Stroebe — *Dieting, Overweight, and Obesity: Self-Regulation in a Food-Rich Environment.* Washington, DC: American Psychological Association, 2008.

Gary Taubes — *Why We Get Fat and What to Do About It.* New York: Alfred A. Knopf, 2011.

Jonathan C.K. Wells — *The Evolutionary Biology of Human Body Fatness: Thrift and Control.* New York: Cambridge University Press, 2010.

Nerys Williams — *Managing Obesity in the Workplace.* New York: Radcliffe, 2008.

Index

Geographic headings and page numbers in **boldface** refer to viewpoints about that country or region.